Core Objectiv

in 24 Hours

**A complete introduction to
Objective-C programming on
the Mac OS X and iOS platforms**

Keith Lee

Core Objective-C *in 24 Hours*

ISBN: 978-1-105-42271-3

The source code for examples that accompany this book, as well as other resources, is available at **www.motupresse.com**.

To batgirl and the curly-haired kid

For your love, support, and positive energy

Contents

About the Author

Keith Lee is a Software Architect and Engineer who has been implementing software systems for over 20 years. He has a vast range of experience implementing desktop applications, distributed (server-side) systems, and software for mobile devices. In addition to his IT pursuits, Keith is also a composer and practicing musician whose works have been performed in the USA and internationally.

Prologue

Core Objective-C *in 24 Hours* provides a clear and concise overview of the programming language, describes its key features and APIs, and presents recommendations for developing Objective-C programs on the Mac. Within 24 hours, the reader will have a solid understanding of Objective-C and be ready to begin using it on his/her projects.

So, let's begin!

Chapter 1
Introduction

Objective-C is the primary programming language for developing applications on Apple's Mac OS X and iOS (iPod, iPhone, iPad) platforms. In recent years these platforms have become some of the most popular development environments for programmers. A key reason for their success is due, in fact, to the features of the Objective-C language itself. General users and IT professionals alike want to be able to quickly grasp the fundamentals of this technology and begin using it to build solutions. This book was written to help you acquire this knowledge by answering the following questions: 1) What do you need to know to understand the Objective-C language and its role within the Mac platforms?, 2) what do you need to begin developing Objective-C programs on the Mac?, and 3) how do you quickly transition to Objective-C from another programming language? **Core Objective-C** *in 24 Hours* provides these answers.

How to Use This Book

This book is divided into two parts. **Part One** provides an introduction to object-oriented programming with Objective-C, describes the software development environment for the Mac OS X and iOS platforms, and summarizes key features of the language. **Part Two** is more focused on application development - it features an in-depth look at the principal components of Objective-C programs, along with a detailed review of the key frameworks and services used for Objective-C application development. The

Appendix contains additional details on the language along with some useful recommendations for programming with Objective-C.

Readers who want a general understanding of Objective-C technology on the Mac will probably focus more on Part One of the book (the *Getting Started, Key Features,* and *Developer Tools* chapters). Experienced developers looking to transition to Objective-C will tend to concentrate on Part Two (the *Application Structure* and *Key Frameworks* chapters along with the Appendix).

Chapter 2
Getting Started

How do you get started with a new programming language? The first steps include acquiring a basic understanding of the language and its key features, along with knowledge of the infrastructure, facilities and tools available for software development. We'll start to lay this foundation here.

Programming Language

Brad Cox and Tom Love created the Objective-C programming language in the early 1980s, with the primary goal of adding object-oriented extensions to the C programming language. Objective-C is actually a strict superset of ANSI C that has been extended with features to support object-oriented programming. These features (object orientation, dynamic types, and reflection) were derived from the Smalltalk programming language.

In 1996 Apple acquired NeXT Software; the NeXTstep/OPENSTEP system served as the basis for the current Apple operating system (Mac OS X). NeXTstep also provided built-in support for the Objective-C language.

Apple released the current version (2.0) of Objective-C in 2007. It added many new features to the language, including automatic memory management (garbage collection), declared and synthesized properties, dot notation, fast enumeration, exception support, runtime performance improvements, and 64-bit machine support.

The *Object* in Objective-C

Object-Oriented Programming (OOP), the motivation for the Objective-C language (i.e. the *Object* in Objective-C), is a style of structured programming that uses objects as the software's key logical elements. An object is a self-contained software entity; it is composed of both state (data) and behavior (operations). The operations that can be performed on an object include accessing and/or updating its data elements, performing computations (e.g. implementing algorithms, etc.), and invoking operations on other objects. At runtime an object-oriented program executes its logic by creating object instances and invoking the desired operations on these objects. In a nutshell, object-oriented software can be viewed as a collection of interacting objects.

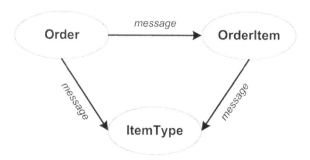

Figure 1. Object Interaction

You develop object-oriented software by structuring application logic as *classes*. A class functions as a specification that is used to dynamically create class instances, i.e. objects.

OrderItem
Data: - description   - quantity   - itemType
Operations: - getDescription   - setQuantity   - getItemType   - computePrice

Figure 2. Anatomy of a Class

OOP simplifies the development of classes through object-oriented concepts such as subtyping (specifying a class based on the data and operations of another class, also known as *inheritance*) and composition (specifying a class based on combinations of other classes).

As an example, let's say you need to develop a program that will manipulate and draw geometric shapes. You can begin by using object-oriented design to develop a Shape class that has, at a minimum, operations to position and draw itself. You can then extend this program (by using inheritance) to develop classes for more specific shapes (e.g. a Circle or a Square) that have additional data (radius, length, and height variables) and operations (compute area, compute circumference).

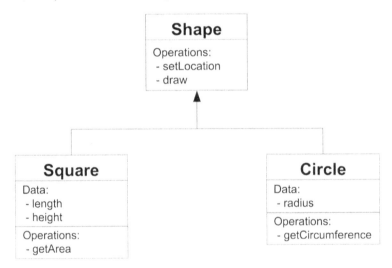

Figure 3. Developing Class Hierarchies

The object-based programming abstraction is an ideal vehicle for creating discrete software units that almost naturally lend themselves to the modeling of logical concepts or physical entities. At its core, developing object-oriented software is all about building a network of interacting objects to implement a problem solution in software. This programming style is valuable for many reasons, not the least of which is support for the direct mapping of real-world concepts and things onto software. Thus OOP facilitates the development of software solutions in line with business goals/problems, and also lends itself to the development of larger, more complex software systems. This type of software development is a key feature enabled by higher-level programming languages such as Objective-C.

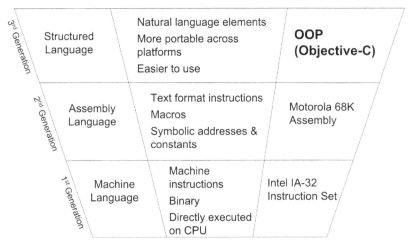

Figure 4. Programming Styles

The practical benefits of object-oriented software development include: 1) code reuse (objects can reused "as is" or combined with other objects to create more complex software components), 2) extensibility (objects can be extended to create new objects), 3) maintainability (if designed properly objects should have minimal coupling with other system components, thus minimizing the impact of change/updates), 4) functional decomposition (object-oriented programming facilitates breaking up large, complex problems into small, more manageable objects), and 5) conceptualization (simpler mapping from the problem space to the solution space, as objects can be designed to represent real entities). Apple has developed a complete set of tools and infrastructure for object-oriented software programming using Objective-C; we'll look at these next.

Development Environment

The development environment for the Mac OS X and iOS platforms greatly simplifies software development, operation, and maintenance. It includes a collection of software development tools, the Objective-C programming language, reusable software components, and the runtime environment. The development environment is used to build Objective-C programs that run on a target platform, currently either a Mac OS X-based computer or a Mac iOS-based device (e.g. an iPad, iPhone, iPod).

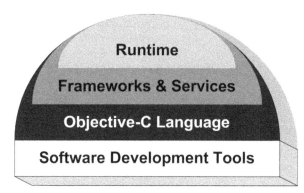

Figure 5. Objective C Software Development Environment

The runtime system provides the environment in which Objective-C programs execute. It enables the dynamic programming capabilities of the language.

The reusable software components (covered in the **Frameworks and Services** chapter) include a set of frameworks, libraries, and services that provide general-purpose functionality to simplify application development. This software provides, *out-of-the-box,* much of the functionality needed to develop applications on the Mac OS X and iOS platforms.

The software development tools (discussed in the **Developer Tools** chapter) enable source code editing and compilation, user interface development, version control, project management, test and debug, and other features. They also simplify application development and enable developers to be more efficient when developing, managing, and maintaining Objective-C software.

Chapter **3**
Developer Tools

Apple has a comprehensive set of tools for Objective-C programming. There are also numerous open-source and 3rd party tools available. This section provides a brief description of these tools.

Mac SDK

The Mac SDK, included with Xcode, is a collection of frameworks, libraries, services, and tools necessary to develop applications that run on the Mac OS X platform. It includes the Cocoa frameworks (AppKit), Application (media) Services, the Foundation framework, and OS X kernel support.

iOS SDK

The iOS SDK, included with Xcode, is a collection of frameworks, libraries, services, and tools necessary to develop software for iOS devices (iPod, iPhone, iPad). The iOS SDK includes the Cocoa Touch frameworks (UIKit), Application (media) Services, the Foundation framework, and iOS kernel support.

Xcode

Xcode is a complete Integrated Development Environment (IDE) for Objective-C software development on the Mac. Xcode is fully integrated with both iOS and Mac OS X; it includes the tools necessary for writing and compiling source code, developing sophisticated user interfaces, software testing and debugging, release build and version management, project management, and a host of other features. Xcode 4, the current release, is a free download for all members of the Apple iOS and Mac Developer Programs. If you are not a member of either program, Xcode 4 for Mac OS X Lion is also available as a free download from the Mac App Store. The next few paragraphs provide an overview of the main features of Xcode 4. For more information, please refer to the Xcode 4 documentation provided at the Mac OS X and iOS Developer Library websites.

Source Editor

The Xcode source editor has a complete set of capabilities for software development and maintenance. These features include automatic formatting, code completion and correction, and online documentation.

The LLVM Compiler 3.0 is specifically tuned for Objective-C programs deployed on the Mac OS X and iOS platforms. It compiles faster than the legacy GCC compiler and also produces applications that can (in some cases) run faster. It also includes several improvements to Objective-C support; these will be discussed in the following chapters.

The Xcode *Fix-it tool* (available when using the LLVM compiler) checks symbols and code syntax while you type, highlights errors, and fixes errors if requested. The editor provides a variety of refactoring operations to improve code structure and simplify maintenance.

UI Editor

Interface Builder (IB) is used for the development of user interfaces for Mac OS X applications and iOS devices. In previous versions of Xcode, Interface Builder was a separate product. Beginning with Xcode version 4, IB is fully integrated into the IDE, thereby making it possible to write and edit source code and tie it directly to your user interface without leaving the Xcode workspace window.

Debugging

Xcode supports two different debuggers, GDB and LLDB, for Objective-C programs. Xcode also includes Clang, a static code analyzer that is used to examine and find potential problems with program logic.

Xcode comes with several additional tools, collectively known as Xcode *Instruments,* which provide further application debugging capabilities. The *Allocations* and *Leaks* instruments are good for tracking down bugs such as memory leaks. The *Zombies* instrument detects attempts to access objects no longer available in memory. The *Time Profiler* instrument can be used to measure Objective-C application performance on iOS devices. The *Energy Diagnostics* instrument enables field-testing of Objective-C applications in near real-world scenarios. The data collected can later be analyzed to tune application performance.

Build Management

Xcode includes the *Schemes* tool for build management. It enables developers to create, edit, and manage software build targets, build configurations to use, and specify the executable environment to use when a target is launched.

Version Editor

The Version Editor provides the capability to manage versions of a software project; it provides integrated support for the Git and Subversion tools used for Source Code Management (SCM).

Project Management

The Projects Editor includes tools for the creation of a single Xcode project or multiple related projects. Xcode provides a *workspace* feature for creating a container of multiple projects that can be used to group Xcode projects and other related files. All the projects in the workspace share the same build directory. The Projects Editor also provides new project options for creating a local source code repository, generation of template unit tests, and adding core data modeling.

iOS Simulator

The iOS simulation environment enables developers to build and run iPod, iPhone, or iPad applications on a Mac computer. Xcode automatically installs an application on the iOS Simulator when it is built targeting the simulation environment. The iOS Simulator is used to find and fix major problems in an application during design and early testing, deploy and test the application UI, and provide an early measure of an application's memory usage.

Data Management

The Xcode data model editor enables the graphical design and development of object data models. The Core Data framework supports the creation, management, and persistence of data model objects, and provides disk-based persistent store types, an in-memory store, and a binary (atomic) store. The data model editor can be used to graphically implement or modify Core Data models, or create mappings between data stores.

OCUnit

OCUnit is an open source unit-testing framework for Objective-C. It is based on SUnit, a unit test framework developed for Smalltalk. Test cases are written in Objective-C and include assertions about the code under test. OCUnit provides the capability to create test suites, collections of test cases that are run uniformly by a test runner, thereby facilitating automatic regression testing. OCUnit is tightly integrated with Xcode; it makes it very easy to create unit tests (configured via a simple check box selection in new Xcode projects).

3rd Party Tools

There are a variety of 3rd party tools available for developing Objective-C software. The next few paragraphs will provide an overview of several of the more popular tools, specifically tools for software compilation and debugging (GCC, GDB), build management (Subversion), and test (OCUnit, OCMock, CoverStory). This list is by no means exhaustive, many other tools are available and it is recommended for the reader to search online for Mac Objective-C developer tools under the categories of interest.

GCC

The GNU Compiler Collection (GCC) is an open source compiler system that supports multiple programming languages, including Objective-C. The current version (GCC v4.6.1) supports all of the features of Objective-C 2.0.

GDB

The GNU Debugger (GDB) is the primary tool used to debug Objective-C code compiled with GCC. GDB provides features to control execution of a program being debugged, stop a program being debugged on specific conditions, examine what has happened when the program has stopped, and change things in a program being debugged, for error detection and correction.

GHUnit

GHUnit is another open source unit-testing framework for Objective-C. It includes several features not provided by OCUnit (control over the number of test cases that are run [all test cases, a subset, just the failed tests], a test runner application that shows passing and failing tests), and is thus may be used in lieu of OCUnit when these features are of particular importance.

OCMock

OCMock is an Objective-C implementation of mock objects. OCMock fully utilizes the dynamic runtime capabilities of Objective-C. It provides capabilities to create, at runtime, mock objects that simulate the behavior of real objects in controlled ways in order to unit test some other (test) object. Mock objects created with OCMock contain assertions that can be used to verify (test) object interactions. For the iOS platform OCMock supports both logic tests (unit tests) and application tests (run on actual device).

CoverStory

CoverStory is a GUI *code coverage* tool; it is used for analyzing which lines of code have actually been executed when running unit tests. It has full AppleScript support, and allows you to export data as HTML. It uses gcov to perform the actual source code analysis.

gcov

gcov is a testing tool that is used for both source test coverage and profiling. Used in conjunction with a unit test tool, gcov can be used to determine how much of the software is tested by a unit test suite. gcov can also be used to find out basic performance statistics such as how often each line of code executes, what lines of code are actually executed, and how much computing time each section of code uses. gcov is integrated into Xcode and works with the GCC compiler.

Chapter **4**

Key Features

Objective-C provides object messaging, encapsulation, single inheritance, and polymorphism features to support object-oriented programming. Its runtime system augments this with dynamic programming capabilities. Enhanced memory management capabilities (automatic reference counting, garbage collection) simplify application development without sacrificing performance. We will now explain these features in more detail and how they are used to develop applications.

Object Messaging

Object messaging enables objects to collaborate by passing messages between themselves. In effect, Objective-C code (e.g., a class/object method or a function) sends a message to a receiving object *(the receiver)* and the receiver uses the message to invoke its corresponding method, returning a result if required.

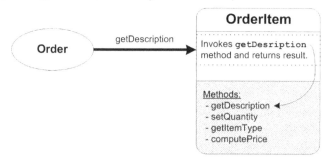

Figure 6. Messaging Passing

15

The type for the message receiver can either be specified in the code and statically bound at compile time (static typing) or unspecified with its type resolved at runtime (dynamic typing). In either case, at runtime the receiving object interprets the message to determine which method to invoke. Objective-C is a dynamically typed language; a byproduct of this is that the receiver is not guaranteed to be able to respond to a message. If it cannot, it will either invoke custom user-defined logic to handle this scenario or raise a runtime exception.

This model of object-oriented programming differs from that used by some OOP languages that employ a *static, compile-time binding* approach for binding a message to the method invoked by an object. Objective-C object messaging with dynamic typing and dynamic binding provides tremendous flexibility with its dynamic programming features; these capabilities enable the development of modular applications that can be modified and/or updated during program execution.

Because Objective-C method calls are resolved at runtime, there is a certain amount of overhead associated with dynamic binding. The Mac Objective-C runtime system caches method calls, saving the message-to-method association in memory, to reduce this overhead.

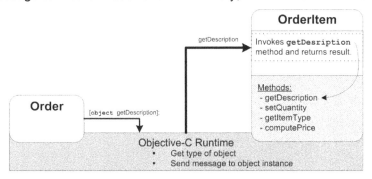

Figure 7. Dynamic Binding

Runtime resolution of method calls provides a great deal of flexibility and extensibility for Objective-C programs, but also comes with some risk: it permits the sending of a message to an object that may not respond. The default response to this condition is for the runtime to throw an exception. Objective-C also provides another mechanism, known as *message forwarding,* which enables an object to perform processing to handle this scenario.

The NSObject class (from the Foundation framework) includes a method, forwardInvocation:, that can be used to implement message forwarding. In the class definition for an object you simply inherit the NSObject class and implement the `forwardInvocation:` method. Subsequently, during application execution if a message is sent to this object that it does not implement, the runtime will invoke the `forwardInvocation:` method for the object.

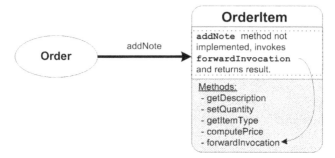

Figure 8. Message Forwarding

The default implementation of the `forwardInvocation:` method from the `NSObject` class simply causes a runtime error to be thrown. By overriding the `NSObject` implementation, a class can implement custom logic.

Message forwarding enables an object to perform a variety of logic on any unrecognized message it receives, perhaps parceling it out to a different receiver who can respond to the message, sending any unrecognized messages to the same destination, or simply silently "swallowing" the message (i.e. performing no processing nor causing a runtime error to be thrown).

Encapsulation

In OOP encapsulation refers to the grouping together of data and operations on that data, along with the ability to restrict access to some of an object's data and/or operations. The latter is also referred to as *information hiding.* Encapsulation is a key to minimizing the interdependencies between software modules. Users of a class interact with it through its methods (via message passing) and are not exposed to implementation details. Encapsulation also improves data integrity, as information hiding prevents users from directly accessing an object's data and potentially setting this data to an invalid or inconsistent state.

Objective-C provides support for both data encapsulation and information hiding. The interface, protocol, category, and implementation class elements are used to provide a well-defined specification for a class that combines all of its data and operations.

Objective-C also includes several modifiers that are used to restrict/prevent direct access to data, specifically instance variables declared in an interface. The modifiers are @private, @protected, and @public. The @private modifier can be applied on member variables and restricts access to instances of the same class. The @protected modifier restricts access to instances of the same class and its subclasses. The @public modifier enables an instance variable to be accessed by any object.

Polymorphism

The word polymorphism is derived from the Greek language and means *having several different forms.* In object-oriented programming polymorphism refers to a programming language's ability to process objects differently depending on their data type or class. Objective-C provides support for polymorphic behavior, specifically, *subtype* polymorphism.

Subtype (or inclusion) polymorphism can be defined as the ability to redefine a method in a child class (i.e. subclass) that has already been defined in its parent (i.e. base) class. The reason this is so beneficial is that it facilitates the creation of class hierarchies whose methods can be invoked from a common interface. Hence the calling object does not need to know the type of the receiver object; and modifications to the class hierarchy (addition of new subclasses, redefinition of methods, etc.) can be performed without impact to the calling object. For example, the class hierarchy depicted below specifies a class hierarchy with a base class (Mammal) that includes the operation getDiet.

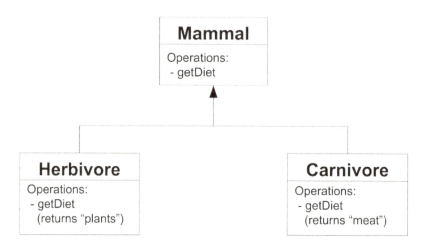

Figure 9. Using Subtype Polymorphism

The subclasses of the `Mammal` class (`Herbivore` and `Carnivore`) redefine the `getDiet` operation (i.e. method) to return an appropriate value. Using polymorphism, code can be written to invoke the method(s) of objects in this class hierarchy using the methods defined in the base class; at runtime the appropriate method will be invoked depending upon the type of the object that receives the message. This makes it possible to disregard the specialized class details of an object family by masking them with a common interface (as specified in the basic class). Objective-C supports subtype polymorphism through the development of class hierarchies and runtime type resolution (via the `id` type) to dynamically invoke the appropriate method at runtime.

Inheritance

Inheritance is a feature of object-oriented programming that enables the development of new classes based on previously defined classes. This new class inherits the state (data) and behavior (methods) of the pre-existing class. The new class is termed the subclass (or derived class) while the pre-existing class is referred to as the superclass or parent class. Objective-C supports single inheritance of both attributes and behavior; hence a class can have only one parent. Objective-C **protocols** also enable a class to support multiple inheritance of interface specification. Almost all Objective-C classes (both existing frameworks/APIs from the Cocoa and Cocoa Touch frameworks along with those developed by the programmer) inherit from the Foundation `NSObject` class.

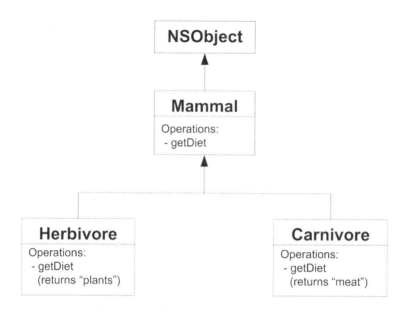

Figure 10. Example Class Hierarchy

Dynamic Runtime

Objective-C shifts much of the responsibility for type, message, and method resolution to the runtime, rather than compile or link time. These capabilities can be used to facilitate developing and updating programs both in real-time, without the need to recompile and re-deploy software, and over time, with minimal or no impact to the existing software.

Dynamic Typing

Dynamic typing enables the determination of the type of an object at runtime; thereby letting runtime factors dictate what kind of object is to be used in your code. This is particularly beneficial when it isn't known in advance what type of object needs to be assigned to a variable, such as when passing arguments to methods. The `id` data type makes this possible through type substitution, as shown in the following code fragment

```
@interface Mammal : NSObject
{
  id species;
}

- (NSString *) getDiet;
- (void) setSpecies: (id) type;
@end
```

Dynamic typing permits associations between objects to be determined at runtime rather than forcing them to be encoded in a static design. Static type checking at compile time may ensure stricter data integrity, but in exchange for that stricter integrity, dynamic typing gives your program much greater flexibility. To partially mitigate this loss of static type checks, Objective-C also provides APIs for runtime object introspection (for example, asking a dynamically typed, anonymous object what its class is). This enables the runtime to verify the type of an object and thus validate its suitability for a particular operation.

Dynamic Binding

Dynamic binding is the process of mapping a message to a method at runtime (i.e. dynamically), rather than at compile-time (i.e. statically). In effect, the message and the object receiving the message aren't set until the program is running and the message is sent. Since the same method could be implemented by potentially many (receiver) objects, the exact method invoked can vary dynamically. Dynamic binding allows new objects and code to be interfaced with or added to a system without affecting existing code, therefore decreasing coupling between objects. It also enables a reduction in program complexity by eliminating the need for conditional logic to handle multiple-choice scenarios (typically implemented with a `switch` statement). Dynamic binding implies the use of dynamic typing, as illustrated in the following code fragment.

```
id mammal = [[Carnivore alloc] init];
NSLog(@"This mammal eats %@", [mammal getDiet]);
```

Dynamic binding is an inherent feature of Objective-C and doesn't require any special APIs. Dynamic binding even allows the message that's sent (the message *selector*) to be a variable determined at runtime.

Dynamic Loading

Dynamic loading, also known as dynamic method resolution, enables an Objective-C program to load both executable code and resources, as they are needed, instead of having to load all program components at application startup. The executable code (which is linked prior to loading) can contain new classes that become integrated into the runtime image of the program. This *lazy-loading* of program code and resources improves overall performance by placing lower memory demands on the system. This also enhances program extensibility, as new software can be added dynamically without change to an existing program.

Memory Management

When developing a program, it is important to manage system resources properly. Objective-C provides three methods for managing memory - *classic memory management, automatic reference counting*, and *automatic memory management*. An Objective-C program that uses classic memory management implements custom logic for cleaning up (i.e. releasing) objects. Automatic reference counting relies on the compiler to automatically add the necessary memory cleanup calls during program compilation. An Objective-C program that uses automatic memory management uses a **garbage collector** to automatically cleanup objects that are no longer being used. Garbage collection is not available for applications deployed on the iOS platform; also note that any C language structures created in an Objective-C program are not available for garbage collection and thus must be managed using automatic reference counting or classic memory management techniques.

Classic Memory Management

With classic memory management the programmer is directly responsible for the cleanup of objects. It is crucial for this logic to be implemented properly; otherwise a program can have memory leaks or attempt to access an object that no longer exists. The overriding guideline for classic memory management is *only release objects you own.* Other, scarce resources (such as file descriptors, network connections, etc.) should be cleaned up immediately when no longer in use. Classic memory management techniques typically used with software developed for the iOS platform and when creating C language data types (i.e., C language structures defined using the malloc function), as this data will not be garbage collected. The

Appendix provides further details on classic memory management (also known as manual retain-release [MRR]), along with practical tips and recommendations.

Automatic Reference Counting

Automatic Reference Counting (ARC) is a new method of memory management that employs reference counting, as with classical memory management, but relies on the compiler to automatically add the necessary memory cleanup calls during program compilation. ARC is now the Apple-recommended approach for memory management on new Objective-C projects. The **Appendix** gives a thorough overview of ARC and how to use it for memory management on both new and existing projects.

Automatic Memory Management

Objective-C 2.0 includes garbage collection technology that is used to automatically manage application memory. All objects are garbage collected; there is no need to explicitly manage objects to prevent memory leaks or avoid access to an object that no longer exists. This reduces the amount of code to be written and maintained, allows the developer to focus on business problem rather than low-level infrastructure services, and also can make it easier to write multi-threaded code. The garbage collector runs as a separate, low-priority thread and consumes minimal system resources. The Objective-C runtime, and hence all Mac Objective-C frameworks and services (along with client code), is a client of the garbage collector:

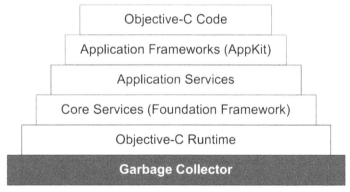

Figure 11. Garbage Collector High-Level Architecture

Garbage collection is enabled by setting the appropriate flag (at compilation) to use the collector. As noted above, the garbage collector is not available for Objective-C applications that run on the Mac iOS platform.

Chapter 5
Application Structure

In the first part of the book we provided an overview of the Objective-C language, the Mac software development environment, and its key features. Now it's time to look at the structure of Objective-C software in greater detail by examining some code! Let's start with the simple program depicted below.

```
//
// OrderItem.h header file
//
#import <Foundation/Foundation.h>

@interface OrderItem : NSObject
  {
    @private NSString *comment;
    @private float price;
  }
  @property (nonatomic, retain) NSString *comment;
  @property float price;

  - (id) initWithComment:(NSString *)cmt price:(float)cost;
@end
```

Figure 12. OrderItem Class Interface

```
//
// OrderItem.m implementation file
//
#import "OrderItem.h"

@implementation OrderItem
  @synthesize comment;
  @synthesize price;

  - (id) initWithComment:(NSString *)cmt price:(float)cost
  {
    self = [super init];
    if (self)
    {
      [self setComment:cmt];
      [self setPrice:cost];
    }
    return self;
  }

- (void)dealloc
{
  [comment release];
  [super dealloc];
}
@end
```

Figure 13. OrderItem Class Implementation

```
//
// main.m OrderItem main
//
#import "OrderItem.h"
#import <Foundation/Foundation.h>

int main(int argc, const char * argv[])
{
  NSAutoreleasePool *pool = [[NSAutoreleasePool alloc] init];

  // Create OrderItems and display some data
  OrderItem *item1 = [[OrderItem alloc] initWithComment:@"Hamburger"
    price:3.50];
  OrderItem *item2 = [[OrderItem alloc] initWithComment:@"Hot dog"
    price:2.75];
  NSLog(@"First item is a %@ for $%.2f", item1.comment, item1.price);
  NSLog(@"Second item is a %@ for $%.2f", item2.comment, item2.price);

  [item2 release];
  [item1 release];
  [pool drain];
  return 0;
}
```

Figure 14. main() Function for OrderItem

The program consists of three files, *OrderItem.h, OrderItem.m,* and *main.m. OrderItem.h,* the *header* file, contains the interface for the `OrderItem` class. OrderItem.m contains the `OrderItem` class implementation. The *main.m* file contains the `main()` function, the entry point for the program. Overall, an Objective-C program includes a combination of preprocessor elements, variables, classes, and functions. It may also be interspersed with C language constructs. The remainder of this chapter will discuss these items in detail.

Preprocessor Elements

The preprocessor is used to transform portions of Objective-C code before compilation. These transformations are made through preprocessing language statements. The Objective-C preprocessor is an extension of the preprocessor provided by the ANSI C programming language – it adds several directives and also supports precompiled header files.

The preprocessing language consists of *directives* to be executed and *macros* to be expanded; a macro can be thought of as one or more abbreviations for program code. The key preprocessor capabilities are:

- *Inclusion of header files*
  The `#import` directive is specific to the Objective-C preprocessor and is used to import header files. Header files provide declarations that can be substituted into the program. As opposed to the `#include` directive that is part of the C preprocessor, the `#import` directive ensures that a file is only included once, thereby preventing recursive includes.

- *Macro expansions*
  Macros are abbreviations for arbitrary fragments of Objective-C code. The preprocessor will perform a literal substitution of the macros with their definitions. Macros are created with the `#define` directive and removed with the `#undef` directive.

- *Conditional compilation*
  These directives enable parts of a program to be included or excluded according to various conditions. The conditional compilation directives are `#if`, `#elif`, `#else`, `#endif`, `#ifdef`, and `#ifndef`.

- *Operators*
  The preprocessor provides several operators that can be used to create string constants and concatenate tokens. The `#` operator is used to create a string literal for the text of macro arguments. The `##` operator is used to concatenate tokens.

- *Diagnostics*
  The preprocessor has several directives for logging errors. The `#error` directive can be used to log a fatal error and halt processing. The `#warning` directive is used to issue a warning and continue processing.

- *Pragmas*
  The `#pragma` directive provides a means for an Objective-C program to provide additional information to the compiler, beyond what is conveyed in the language itself. If the compiler doesn't recognize the directive, it ignores it. For Objective-C programs developed using Xcode, `#pragma` directives provide a means of logically organizing Objective-C code to make the IDE more efficient to use.

Variables

Objective-C data is most commonly manipulated using variables. A variable is a container for a value; it completely defines a data element according to its type, scope, accessibility, and type-specific optional features.

Variable Types

There are multiple data types used in an Objective-C program. These include standard *basic* types, types inherited from ANSI C, and types specific to Objective-C. The basic types are `int` (an integer number), `float` (a floating-point number), `double` (a large floating-point *number*), and `char` (a single character). Qualifiers can be placed before some of these basic types (e.g. `long`, `long long`, `short`, `unsigned`, `signed`) to change their length and/or properties. For example, the syntax to declare a long integer is

```
long int myInt;
```

As another example, the syntax to declare a floating-point number and initialize it to a value of 3.5 is

```
float myFloat = 3.5;
```

The most common ANSI C types are discussed in the chapter on C Language Features; they are the `array`, `structure`, and `pointer` data types.

Objective-C has several unique data types, the most common of which are the `id`, `BOOL`, and `SEL` types. The `id` type can be considered as a generic object type; it is used to store a reference (i.e., a *pointer,* the address in memory) to any object. For example, the declaration

```
id hello;
```

declares hello to be a variable of type `id`. In other words `hello` is a pointer to an object instance in memory. The type (e.g., class) of the object is not specified statically, but rather is determined at runtime (via dynamic typing). The `BOOL` (or `_Bool`) data type is used for handling true or false (1 or 0) conditions. `SEL` is a data type used to refer to the name of a method. It is used to invoke a method on an object, potentially varying the method at runtime via dynamic binding. The `@selector` directive is used to refer to a `SEL` data type instance. For example, you can retrieve the selector of a method named *greetings* that has no arguments with the statement

```
SEL greetingSelector = @selector(greetings:);
```

You could then invoke the `greetings` method (i.e. send a message) on an object instance (in this example the *hello* object) with the statement

```
[hello performSelector:greetingSelector];
```

Selectors make it possible to dynamically vary the message sent to an object at runtime.

Variable Scope

The visibility and accessibility of a variable is a function of its scope. They may exist and be visible within a statement block of a method, within an object instance (or related objects), throughout a file, across all object instances of a class, or across multiple files. Instance variables are declared within a class interface; the associated access modifier specifies their scope. Variables declared outside of an implementation in a class implementation file are shared between all object instances of the class, but are not visible elsewhere. Variables declared outside of an interface in a class header file are shared across and visible to all object instances of the class, as well as any interface/class/etc. that imports the header.

Variable Retention

The `static` and `extern` keywords modify the scope and retention of variables. The `static` keyword states that a variable is initialized at the start of program execution and that its value is retained. This keyword is typically used to create a variable declared at file level that is retained and can be referenced anywhere within the file. The statement

```
static int counter = 0;
```

if declared at file level (i.e., outside any implementation section within a class implementation file), creates a variable named `counter` that can be referenced anywhere within the corresponding file. The value of the variable can be retrieved and/or updated (by class method definitions, etc.) anywhere within the file.

The `extern` keyword states that a variable is being declared in a statement, but will be defined elsewhere. It is used to facilitate sharing and prevent multiple definitions of a variable. The statement

```
extern int myArg;
```

declares `myArg` as an external variable of type `int` that is defined elsewhere, typically in another file that is part of the overall application.

Access Modifiers

Objective-C includes several directives to control the scope of instance variables, i.e. the visibility of variables throughout a program. This is declared with the `@public`, `@private`, `@protected`, and `@package` modifiers. The `@public` directive indicates that the instance variable is accessible everywhere. The `@protected` directive indicates that the instance variable is accessible within the class that declares it and within classes that inherit it. This is the default scope. The `@private` directive specifies that the instance variable is accessible only within the class that declares it. The `@package` directive specifies that an instance variable has `@public` scope inside the linked program/framework/library, but `@private` scope outside of it. The following (class interface) instance variable declaration

```
{
  @public int counter;
  @protected float temperature;
  @private NSString *description;
}
```

Declares a `counter` variable of type `int` that is accessible everywhere, a `temperature` variable of type `float` that is accessible within the declaring class and any subclasses, and a `description` variable of type `NSString*` that is accessible only within the declaring class.

The Class Section

Classes are the fundamental elements of object-oriented programming; hence the class sections typically contain the majority of the code of an Objective-C program. A class is completely specified by its interface and implementation. It may also implement a category and/or one or more protocols.

Interface

An interface declares the instance variables (data) and methods (behavior) of a class. The methods declared by an interface specify the messages that can be sent to an object. The parent class, if any, is also declared in the interface section.

Syntactically an interface declaration begins with the `@interface` keyword and the name of the class. It ends with the `@end` keyword. Class inheritance is specified by appending the `@interface` keyword with a colon (`:`) delimiter followed by the name of the corresponding parent class. Between these statements instance variables are declared (within a block of code surrounded by curly braces), followed by property and method declarations. The overall syntax of an interface declaration is thus

```
@interface ClassName : Parent
{
  Instance variable declarations
}
  Property declarations
  Method declarations
@end
```

Protocol

A protocol declares methods that can be implemented by any class. As shown above in the chapter on Interfaces, an interface is directly associated with a specific class and hence a class hierarchy. Because a protocol is not associated with any particular class it can be used to capture similarities among classes that are not hierarchically related. In addition, in contrast to an interface, a protocol does not declare instance variables. Protocols provide Objective-C with the capability to support the concept of multiple inheritance of specification (i.e. of method declarations).

A protocol declaration begins with the `@protocol` keyword followed by the name of the protocol. It ends with the `@end` keyword. Protocols can have both *required* and *optional* methods; optional methods do not require that an implementation of the protocol implement these methods. The keywords `@required` and `@optional` (followed by the method name(s)) are used to mark a method appropriately. If neither keyword is specified, the default behavior is required. The syntax of a protocol declaration is thus

```
@protocol ProtocolName
```
 Property declarations
```
@required
```
  Method declarations
```
@optional
```
  Method declarations
```
@end
```

One protocol can incorporate other protocols by specifying the name of each declared protocol within braces; this is referred to as *adopting* a protocol. Commas are used to separate multiple protocols

```
@protocol ProtocolName <ProtocolName(s)>
```
  Method declarations
```
@end
```

An interface can *adopt* other protocols using similar syntax

```
@interface ClassName : Parent <ProtocolName(s)>
```
  Method declarations
```
@end
```

Category

A category enables the addition of new functionality to an existing class without subclassing it. Categories can also be used to override an existing method, although this **is not** recommended (use a subclass instead). The methods in a category become part of the class type (within the scope of the program) and are inherited by all subclasses. There is no difference at runtime between the original methods and the added methods. This means that you can send a message to any instance of the class (or its subclasses) to invoke a method defined in the category. Typically categories are used: 1) to extend classes defined by others (even if you don't have access to the source code), 2) as an alternative to a subclass, or 3) to distribute the implementation of a new class into multiple source files (this can help simplify the development of a large class being by multiple programmers).

A category interface declaration begins with the `@interface` keyword followed by the name of the existing class, the category name in parentheses, followed by the protocols it adopts (if any). It ends with the `@end` keyword. Between these statements the method declarations are provided. The syntax of a category declaration is thus

```
@interface ClassName (CategoryName) <ProtocolName(s)>
  Method declarations
@end
```

A category declaration is composed of method declarations only; it cannot declare properties. Now let's write the code for a category; earlier in this chapter we looked at an example program (Figures 12-14) that defined an `OrderItem` class. We can write a category that adds a new method named `computePrice:` to this class with the following code (Note: this code lists both the interface and the implementation for a category, we'll talk about class implementations shortly).

```
@interface OrderItem (Compute)
- (float) computePrice: (int) quantity;
@end
@implementation OrderItem (Compute)
- (float) computePrice: (int) quantity
{
  return price * quantity;
}
@end
```

The `Compute` category adds the `computePrice:` method to the `OrderItem` class and any of its subclasses. Note that the category has access to the `OrderItem` member variables, specifically the `price` variable.

An *extension* can be considered as an anonymous (i.e. unnamed) category. The methods declared in an extension **must be** implemented in the main `@implementation` block for the corresponding class (they cannot be implemented in a category). The syntax of a class extension is thus

```
@interface ClassName ()
  Property declarations
  Method declarations
@end
```

As shown in the declaration above, an extension also differs from a category in that it can declare properties. The compiler will verify that the methods (and properties) declared in an extension are implemented. A class extension is commonly placed in the same file as the class implementation file, and is used to group and declare additional required, private methods (e.g. not part of the publicly declared API) for use solely within a class.

Implementation

An implementation defines the class declared by its interface; this consists of defining its properties, the methods declared by its interface, along with the methods declared by any corresponding protocols and categories.

The general syntax for the implementation of a class is

```
@implementation ClassName (CategoryName) <ProtocolName(s)>
  Property definitions
  Method definitions
@end
```

The method definitions contain the actual code for a class. The syntax for properties and methods is defined in upcoming chapters.

Class Updates with LLVM 3.0

The LLVM 3.0 compiler includes several improvements to Objective-C support; specifically it allows instance variables to be declared in class extensions and/or implementations, thereby improving data hiding by eliminating these from the class interface. The syntax for a class extension is thus updated to

```
@interface ClassName()
{
  Instance variable declarations
}
  Property declarations
  Method declarations
@end
```

and the syntax for a class implementation is

```
@implementation ClassName(CategoryName) <ProtocolName(s)>
{
  Instance variable declarations
}
  Property definitions
  Method definitions
@end
```

The Object Lifecycle – Creating Instances of a Class

An Objective-C program manages the lifecycle of objects throughout program execution. Once a class has been declared and defined, an object (an *instance* of a class) is created by first allocating memory for the instance, then initializing it properly. The `alloc` message (method inherited from the root `NSObject` class) is used to allocate memory for an object, for example the statement

```
Molecule *water = [Molecule alloc];
```

dynamically allocates memory for the new `Molecule` object's instance variables and initializes them all to a value of 0. Once created, the `init` message is used to completely initialize the object, e.g.

```
water = [water init];
```

These two steps are typically combined into a single statement

```
Molecule *water = [[Molecule alloc] init];
```

To perform custom initialization logic, the `init` or `initWith` method is implemented. This logic should also include initialization of the parent class, for example of the `Molecule` class is a subclass of `NSObject` the following pseudo-code performs initialization logic for the parent class (`NSObject`) and then custom initialization logic for the `Molecule` class.

```
@implementation Molecule
- (id) init
{
  self = [super init];
  if (self != nil)
  {
    self.name = @"Water";
    self.numberOfAtoms = 3;
  }
}
```

Also note that object instances are always manipulated by pointers; this is true for both object messaging and method invocations. An object instance is not passed as the parameter of a method, but rather a pointer to it.

Properties

A property provides a simple and convenient mechanism for declaring and defining methods to access class instance variables. In many programming languages property (also known as accessor) methods must be manually coded. This increases the amount of code to be developed and maintained, and can also lead to hard to detect errors due to memory management requirements, thread safety requirements, and other concerns. Declared properties address these problems by: 1) providing a clear, explicit specification of how accessor methods behave, and 2) enabling the compiler to generate the accessor methods automatically according to your provided specification (thereby reducing the amount of code to write and maintain). You declare a property for a class instance variable using the `@property` keyword followed by an optional set of attributes (in parentheses), the type and name of the variable

`@property` *(attributes)* **type** `VariableName;`

The optional attributes provide additional details about the storage semantics and other behaviors of the property. Property declarations are typically provided in the interface of a class, but can also be provided in a protocol or category declaration (See the **Appendix** for more information regarding property attributes and declarations). A declared property is instantiated within the corresponding class implementation using the `@synthesize` keyword followed by the name of the variable

`@synthesize VariableName;`

Accessor methods for a property can be overwritten to provide custom logic. The `@dynamic` property directive can also be used to prevent compiler auto-generation of accessor methods. The compiler will not generate a warning if it cannot find implementations of accessor methods associated with the properties whose names follow the `@dynamic` property. Instead, the developer is responsible for writing the accessor method implementations directly or using some other method to derive them (such as dynamic code loading or dynamic method resolution).

Methods

Methods implement the functional logic of a class. Methods can be declared in a class interface, a protocol, and/or a category. Methods declared in one or more of the above are defined in a corresponding class implementation.

A method is declared by specifying the: 1) the method type, 2) its return type, and 3) one or more *method name-parameter* pairs. The following example method declaration will be used to explain the method declaration syntax.

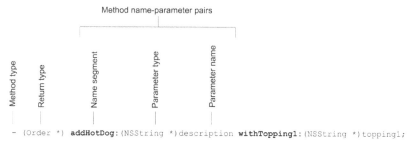

Figure 15. Method Declaration Syntax

The **method type** specifies whether the method is a class or instance method. A class method is declared with a + sign and indicates that the method has class scope, meaning that it operates at the class level and does not have access to the instance variables of the class (unless they are passed as parameters to the method). An instance method is declared with a − sign and indicates that the method has object scope; it operates at the instance level and has access to the instance variables of the object. The example declares an instance method.

The **return type** indicates the type of the returned variable from the method, if any. The return type is specified within parentheses, following the method type. If the method does not return anything, the return type is declared as `void`. In the above example, the method returns a pointer to an `Order` object.

As mentioned above, a method name can be composed of multiple **name-parameter** pairs. Particularly compared to other languages, the syntax surrounding name-parameter pairs can seem confusing. The rationale behind this naming convention is to facilitate the creation of regular, self-descriptive method names that are easy to read and understand. With that in mind, the syntax for each method name-parameter pair is

nameSegment: `(parameterType)parameterName`

A name segment is followed by a colon, the corresponding parameter type (enclosed in parentheses), and the parameter name. In the above example there are two name-parameter pairs − 1) `addHotDog:(NSString *)description` and 2)

withTopping1:(NSString *)topping1. The first name
segment is addHotDog:. Its corresponding parameter is of type
NSString * and is named description. The second name
segment is withTopping1:. Its parameter is of type NSString *
and is named topping1. Note the grammar for the method name
– the first name segment (addHotDog) is comprised of a verb and
direct object, while the second segment (withTopping1) is a
prepositional phrase – Objective-C method names are meant to read
like sentences! This syntax (along with some simple naming
conventions) facilitates the creation of methods whose names are
more self-documenting and easier to understand without having to
thoroughly examine the implementation.

To summarize, the above method declaration specifies an instance
method that returns a pointer to an Order instance whose name is
addHotDog:withTopping1:. Its input parameters are a
description (of type NSString *) and a topping1 (of type
NSString *). The method implementation syntax is identical to
that of the declaration, but instead of a terminating semicolon it is
followed by the implementation logic (method statements)

```
- (Order *) addHotDog:(NSString *)description
    withTopping1:(NSString *)topping1
{
    Method statements
}
```

Invoking Methods – Sending a Message to an Object

An object (the *sender*) interacts with another object (the *receiver*) by
sending it a message, thus causing the receiver to invoke a specific
method. The syntax for invoking a method on an object is

```
[receiver methodNameSegment:parameterValue];
```

where the receiver is a *pointer* to an object instance and the
methodNameSegment(s) define the message sent to the receiver.

If the method has multiple segments its name and parameter values
are listed consecutively, thus for the reference example method
listed previously (addHotDog:withTopping1:) the syntax for
invoking this method on a (receiving) object instance named order1
is

```
[order1 addHotDog:@"Chicago"
  withTopping1:@"onions"];
```

The syntax for invoking a class method replaces the object instance with the class name. Hence for a corresponding `Order` class method the syntax for invoking this method (on an `order1` object instance) is

```
[Order.class addHotDog:@"Chicago"
  withTopping1:@"onions" order:order1];
```

Messages can also be nested, thereby avoiding the use of local variables to store temporary results. The return value from each nested message is used as the target of another message; for example if the `order1` object instance has a method `computeTotal:` which computes the cost of an order, it would be invoked as follows

```
[[order1 addHotDog:@"Chicago"
  withTopping1:@"onions"] computeTotal];
```

The Main Section

The `main()` function is the entry point for an Objective-C program, and is called when the program begins execution. An executable Objective-C program must have a `main()` function. The syntax for the `main()` function is

```
int main(int argc, const char *argv[])
{
    Program code
}
```

The `main()` function has a return type of `int` and two parameters, `argc` of type `int` (the count of the number of input parameters) and an array (`argv`) of pointers to `const char` variables (the actual input parameters for the program). If a program named `order` was compiled and linked, executing the program as shown below

```
root> order hamburger pizza
```

would invoke the `main()` function for the `order` program, passing in the character strings `hamburger` and `pizza` (`argv[0]` and `argv[1]`) as the input parameters. Note that a function is a **C Language Element,** to be discussed in the next chapter.

C Language Elements

As Objective-C is a strict superset of ANSI C, it is possible to freely mix ANSI C code with Objective-C in a program. There are a variety of reasons why this approach is not recommended. C is a procedural programming language, and mixing two programming styles (object-oriented and procedural) in the same program can make the software difficult to understand and maintain. In addition some key features provided by Objective-C, such as automatic memory management, are not supported by C-language structures.

Although it is not recommended to mix the use of C language elements in Objective-C programs, there are scenarios where it makes sense to use C within an Objective-C program. There is also a large body of existing (legacy) C code that you may encounter. This chapter provides a brief overview of some of the more common C language elements along with recommendations on their usage.

Arrays

An array type is a set of ordered data items, all of the same type. An array definition specifies the type of element that will be contained in the array (`int, float, pointer, structure,` *class type*, etc.) and the maximum number of elements that will be stored in it (within brackets).

```
int values[10];
```

Once defined, an array value can be referenced by specifying the array name followed by the index of the value being referenced within brackets.

```
int myValue = values[0];
```

Note this example also shows that array indices start at 0. Arrays can be linear or multidimensional.

Structures

A structure is a complex type that acts as a container for other types. It supports basic types (e.g. `int, float`, etc.), arrays, pointers, other structures, and class types. A structure is defined using the keyword `struct` followed by the structure name, then the declaration of each structure *member* (type and name followed by a semicolon) within curly braces

```
struct time
{
   int hour;
   int minutes;
   float seconds;
}
```

This defines a new type such that variables can now be declared to be of type `struct` *time*.

```
struct time currentTime;
```

Specifying the name of the instance, a period (dot notation), then the member name, accesses a member of a structure instance.

```
currentTime.hour = 8;
```

Like classes, structures encapsulate state (data). They differ from classes in that they do not encapsulate behavior (methods) on the data; also, structures do not have access modifiers (`@private`, `@protected`, `@public`) for data hiding.

Functions

A function has many features in common with an Objective-C method. It is a portion of code that performs a specific task and is capable of being invoked. It has a return type and can take parameters. Also, it is declared and then defined. A function differs from an Objective-C method in that it is not associated with a class type.

In its simplest form a function is declared by specifying its return type, function name, parameter types within parentheses, and a terminating semicolon. For example, a function named `hello` that returns an `int` and has an `int` and a `float` for its parameter types would be declared with the following statement:

```
int hello(int, float);
```

The corresponding function is defined by specifying its return type, function name, parameters within parentheses, and then the implementation code within curly braces:

```
int hello(int ii, float yy)
{
    Implementation code
}
```

Functions are invoked within an Objective-C program by entering within an expression or statement the function name and its parameters (within parentheses):

```
hello(3, 7.5);
```

Pointers

A pointer is a variable that contains the memory address for another variable. It is defined like a normal variable, but with an asterisk before the variable name. The type-specifier determines what kind of variable the pointer points to but does not affect the actual pointer. The statement

```
int *myInt;
```

declares a pointer of type `int`, meaning that `myInt` contains the memory address for an `int` variable. The reference operator `(&)` retrieves the memory address for a variable, thus the following set of statements

```
int *myInt;
int testVal = 10;
myInt = &testVal;
```

declare `myInt` to be a pointer of type `int` that points to the variable `testVal` (which contains a value of 10). To de-reference the variable that a pointer points to in a statement, you prefix the pointer name with an asterisk (indirection). The statement

```
*myInt = 20;
```

changes the value of `testVal` (the variable that `myInt` points to) to 20. Note that the asterisk in a type definition (followed by a variable name) defines a pointer variable, whereas the *indirection* operator (the asterisk before a pointer variable in a statement, as shown above) is used to get/set the contents of a variable (`testVal` above) through its pointer.

Pointers can point to more complex data types, such as arrays or structures. A pointer to a structure has a special operator `(->)` that enables access to member variables of a structure. Given a `struct time` instance named `currentTime`, the following code

```
struct time *timePtr;
timePtr = &currentTime;
timePtr->hour = 8;
```

creates a pointer (`timePtr`) to this instance and sets the value of `hour` in the `currentTime` structure to 8. A pointer to an array points to the type of the element contained in the array. The statements

```
int values[10];
int *valuesPtr;
valuesPtr = values;
```

produce a pointer to the first element of the `values` array. To sequence through the elements of an array with a pointer, you add the increment to the array pointer (surrounded by parentheses), prefixed by the indirection operator to retrieve the value of the array element; the two statements

```
int myValue = *(valuesPtr + 1);
int myValue = values[1];
```

both retrieve the value of the second element in the `values` array (i.e. `values[1]`);

A pointer can be passed as a parameter in a method or function call, and also returned as its result. It is also possible to create a pointer to a function; the syntax for declaring such a pointer is

```
type (*fnPtr) (ParameterTypes);
```

This declares a function pointer named `fnPtr` with a return type of `type` and parameter types named *ParameterTypes*. Therefore if `testFunction` were a function that returned *type* and took the corresponding arguments, the statement

```
fnPtr = testFunction;
```

stores a pointer to this function inside the function pointer variable `fnPtr`. The function can be called by providing its name followed by parentheses, with any arguments to the function inside the parentheses; for example

```
fnPtr(3, 7.5);
```

Chapter **6**

Frameworks and Services

The Mac development environment includes numerous frameworks and services that can be used to facilitate application development. In this chapter we will provide an overview of several key frameworks, illustrated with code examples.

Cocoa and Cocoa Touch

The Cocoa and Cocoa Touch frameworks are comprised of libraries, APIs, and runtimes that form the development layer for the Mac OS X and Mac iOS platforms. The Cocoa frameworks are for Mac OS X programming, whereas the Cocoa Touch frameworks are designed for iOS programs. These frameworks are largely implemented in Objective-C, and hence are directly available for use in Objective-C programs.

Cocoa includes several primary frameworks as well as specialized frameworks. The primary frameworks are Foundation, AppKit (Cocoa), and UIKit (Cocoa Touch). The specialized frameworks and services provide support for audio and video processing, graphics and animation, data management, networking, bridges to scripting languages, user applications, and (for the iOS platform) device access and control.

Foundation Framework

The Foundation framework defines a base layer of APIs that can be used for any type of Objective-C program. It includes the root object class (NSObject), classes for basic data types such as strings, wrapper classes for primitive data types, collection classes for storing and manipulating other objects, classes for system information, classes for networking, and other functionality. The following paragraphs provide an overview of each API along with example code; to become familiar with the complete set of Foundation framework APIs please consult the Apple Foundation Framework Reference Guide.

Value Objects

The Value Object classes implement object-oriented wrappers for primitive data types, along with general-purpose system information, tools, and locale support. The NSCalendar, NSDate, NSCalendarDate, NSDateComponents, and NSTimeZone classes provide support for date and time programming and formatting. The NSValue, NSNumber, NSDecimalNumber and NSDecimalNumberHandler provide object-oriented wrappers for primitive data types, which can then be manipulated and/or added to collection objects. The NSData, NSMutableData, and NSPurgeableData classes provide object-oriented wrappers for byte buffers. NSValueTransformer is used to transform values from one representation to another. NSNull is a singleton object used to represent null values in collection objects that don't allow nil values. NSLocale provides support for *locales,* a collection of information used to adapt software for a specific region or language. NSCache provides an in-memory system cache for the temporary storage of objects that are expensive to recreate.

The following code fragment creates an int variable named seven and stores it as an NSNumber instance

```
int seven = 7;
NSNumber *sevenNumber =
  [NSNumber numberWithInt:seven];
```

You can then retrieve the value as an int

```
int number = [sevenNumber intValue];
```

or get a string representation of the number

```
NSString *sevenStr = [sevenNumber stringValue];
```

Strings

The Strings classes provide general-purpose functionality for creating, formatting, and processing strings. They support the creation of immutable and mutable string objects, attributed strings (strings with attributes such as font, paragraph style, foreground color, etc.), and unicode characters. The formatter classes (`NSFormatter`, `NSDateFormatter`, *and* `NSNumberFormatter`) are used to create, interpret, and validate the textual representation of objects (specifically dates and numbers). `NSScanner` reads and converts `NSString` objects into number and string values. `NSSortDescriptor` provides a mechanism for ordering objects according to a variety of selected parameters.

Given a string literal

```
@"12345 Anywhere Drive"
```

The next statement creates a pointer to an immutable string object (i.e., an `NSString *`) named `streetAddr` and assigns it to this string literal

```
NSString *streetAddr = @"12345 Anywhere Drive";
```

The `NSString` class has numerous methods for obtaining information about the string, for example, to get the length of the string named `streetAddr`

```
int len = [streetAddr length];
```

Collections

The collections classes deliver functionality for managing collections of objects. Most collections have both an immutable and a mutable version. `NSArray` and `NSMutableArray` manage ordered collections of arrays. `NSDictionary` and `NSMutableDictionary` are used for groups of key-value pairs. `NSSet`, `NSMutableSet`, and `NSCountedSet` are used to manage unordered collections of objects. The `NSEnumerator` and `NSDirectoryEnumerator` classes enumerate collections of other objects, such as arrays and dictionaries. `NSIndexSet` and `NSMutableIndexSet` manage collections of *index sets* (collections of unique unsigned integers used to store indexes into another data structure). `NSHashTable`, `NSMapTable`, and `NSPointerArray` are mutable collections that support weak relationships when using the garbage collector. An `NSPointerFunctions` instance is used by an `NSHashTable`, `NSMapTable`, or `NSPointerArray` object to define behavior for the pointers it manages.

The following code fragment stores several `NSNumber` objects in an `NSArray` instance

```
NSNumber *nOne = [NSNumber numberWithInt:1];
NSNumber *nTwo = [NSNumber numberWithInt:2];
NSArray *nArray = [NSArray
   arrayWithObjects: nOne, nTwo, nil];
```

Note that a collection instance is terminated with `nil` to indicate the end of the collection of objects. You can search for an object (with the same value) in the array with the following statement

```
NSUInteger index = [nArray indexOfObject:nTwo];
```

This method returns the index in the array for the object, which can then be retrieved with the statement

```
NSNumber *myNumber = [nArray objectAtIndex:index];
```

The `NSHashTable, NSMapTable, NSPointerArray,` and `NSPointerFunctions` classes are available for use on the Mac OS X platform (i.e., these classes are not available for programs that run on Mac iOS devices - iPhone, iPad, iPod).

XML Processing

The XML processing collection of classes support general-purpose XML document management and parsing functionality. The classes logically represent an XML document as a hierarchical tree structure and support the query and manipulation of XML document nodes. The classes support several XML-related technologies and standards, such as XQuery, XPath, XInclude, XSLT, DTD, and XHTML.

Classes `NSXMLDTD` and `NSXMLDTDNode` are used for creating and modifying XML Document Type Definitions (DTDs). `NSXMLDocument, NSXMLNode,` and `NSXMLElement` are used for processing XML documents. Instances of `NSXMLParser` are used to parse XML documents in an event-driven manner. The following method demonstrates the creation, initialization, and use of an `NSXMLParser` instance to parse an XML document

```
- (void) parseXMLInfoset:(NSString *)file
{
  NSURL *infoset = [NSURL fileURLWithPath:file];
  NSXMLParser *parser = [[NSXMLParser alloc]
    initWithContentsOfURL:infoset];
  [parser setDelegate:self];
  [parser setShouldResolveExternalEntities:YES];
  [parser parse];
}
```

An object must conform to the NSXMLParserDelegate protocol to be able to process document parsing events (e.g., begin parsing document, end parsing document, start parsing element, start mapping namespace prefix, end mapping namespace prefix) from an NSXMLParser instance.

The NSXMLParser class is available on both the Mac OS X and iOS platform; the other XML processing classes mentioned here are only available for use on the Mac OS X platform.

Predicates

This collection of classes provides a general means of specifying queries using predicates and expressions. A *predicate* is a logical operator that returns either a true or false value and is composed of one or more *expressions*. Predicates are used to constrain a search for a query or to provide filtering of returned results. The NSExpression class is used to represent expressions in a predicate, and it supports multiple expression types. NSPredicate, NSComparisonPredicate, and NSCompoundPredicate are used to create predicates. Given the array

```
NSArray *nArray = [NSArray arrayWithObjects:
  [NSNumber 1],[NSNumber 2], nil];
```

The following code fragment creates a predicate that searches for elements in the array with a value greater than 1, and then creates a new, filtered array using this predicate

```
NSPredicate *pred = [NSPredicate
  predicateWithFormat: @"SELF > 1"];
NSArray *filteredArray = [nArray
  filteredArrayUsingPredicate:pred];
```

File I/O

The File I/O classes consist of a collection of APIs for using files and directories. The classes enable you to represent file paths, perform basic operations with files and directories, find directories on the system, and use streams to perform I/O operations. The NSBundle class groups code and resources that can be used in a program. They are used to locate program resources, dynamically load and unload executable code, and assist in localization. NSFileHandle is an object-oriented wrapper for a file descriptor. The NSFileManager class provides methods for performing file-system operations. NSStream, NSInputStream, and NSOutputStream provide functionality for reading from/writing to streams. The NSMetadataItem and NSMetadataQuery set of classes provide APIs for metadata queries.

The NSMetadataItem and NSMetadataQuery classes are only available for use on the Mac OS X platform.

Operating System Services

These classes consist of a variety of infrastructure services and general-purpose APIs. The NSHost class contains methods to access the network name and address information for a host. The NSNetService and NSNetServiceBrowser classes provide information about network services. NSOrthography, NSSpellServer, and NSTextCheckingResult are primarily used for text processing. NSProcessInfo is used to access information about the current process. NSRunLoop declares the interface to objects that manage input sources such as mouse and keyboard events from the window system. The NSTimer class is used to create timers that send a specified message to a target object after a certain time has elapsed. NSUserDefaults provides an API for storing user preferences used to enable an application to customize its behavior. The NSError class encapsulates extensible error information beyond that provided by an error code or string.

The NSSpellServer class is only available for use on the Mac OS X platform.

URL Support

The URL Support classes are used for interacting with URLs and communicating with resources using standard Internet protocols (ftp, http, https, files). They also support proxy servers and SOCKS gateways. The URL loading classes (NSURLResponse, NSHTTPURLResponse, NSURLRequest, NSHTTPURLRequest, NSURLConnection, and NSURLDownload) are used to create a request for the content of a URL and download the response from the resource. The cache management classes (NSURLCache and NSCacheURLRequest) provide a composite disk and in-memory cache for responses to URL requests. The authentication and credentials classes (NSURLProtectionSpace, NSURLCredentialStorage, NSURLCredential, NSURLAuthenticationChallenge, and NSURLAuthenticationChallengeSender) provide support for authenticating users requesting access to protected URLs. The cookie storage classes (NSHTTPCookie and NSHTTPCookieStorage) facilitate the creation and management of HTTP cookies, used to provide persistent storage of data across URL requests. The protocol support classes (NSURLProtocol and NSURLProtocolClient) enable the creation of custom protocols for transferring data.

To download the resource "www.motupresse.com/test.gif" create an NSURLRequest instance for the URL, specifying the cache access policy and timeout interval for the connection

```
NSURLRequest *request = [NSURLRequest
  requestWithURL:
  [NSURL URLWithString:
    @"http://www.motupresse.com/test.gif"]
  cachePolicy:NSURLRequestUseProtocolCachePolicy
  timeoutInterval:60.0];
```

then create the connection, assign the delegate object for the connection, and begin asynchronously downloading the data

```
NSURLConnection *connection =
  [[NSURLConnection alloc]
  initWithRequest:request delegate:self];
```

Note that a run loop for the connection must be started to download the data via the callback methods. It can be started using the NSRunLoop run: method for the current thread

```
[[NSRunLoop currentRunLoop] run];
```

Typically the data being downloaded is stored in an instance variable

```
NSMutableData *receivedData;
if (connection)
```

```
{
  receivedData = [[NSMutableData data] retain];
}
```

The delegate object can implement multiple methods associated with URL request processing. To access the data after it has been successfully downloaded, the delegate should implement the connectionDidFinishLoading: method

```
- (void) connectionDidFinishLoading:
  (NSURLConnection *)connection
{
  NSLog(@"Retrieved %d bytes of data",
    [receivedData length]);
}
```

After the connection is no longer being used, it should be released.

```
[connection release];
```

Interprocess Communication

These classes enable process-to-process communication; specifically they provide facilities for creating and using communication channels. NSPipe supplies an interface for accessing pipes, a one-way channel for communication between processes. NSPort, NSMachPort, NSMessagePort, and NSSocketPort provide low-level mechanisms for communication between threads or processes, typically via NSPortMessage objects. NSPortNameServer, NSMachBootstrapServer, NSMessagePortNameServer, and NSSocketPortNameServer provide an interface to the port registration service, used retrieve instances of NSMachPort, NSMessagePort, and NSSocketPort.

The following code fragment creates a server socket with port number 4444

```
NSSocketPort *serverPort = [[NSSocketPort alloc]
  initWithTCPPort:4444];
```

The server then listens for connections using an NSConnection instance

```
NSConnection *connection = [[NSConnection alloc]
  initWithReceivePort:serverPort sendPort:nil];
```

The NSSocketPort, NSPortMessage, NSPortNameServer, NSMachBootstrapServer, NSMessagePortNameServer, and

`NSSocketPortNameServer` classes are only available for use on the Mac OS X platform.

Threads Support

The Threads Support classes implement functionality that enables concurrent execution of multiple sections of code using threads. `NSLock, NSDistributedLock, NSConditionLock,` and `NSRecursiveLock` are used to create locks for synchronizing code execution. `NSOperation, NSBLockOperation,` and `NSInvocationOperation` are used to manage concurrent execution of one or more *operations,* code and data associated with a single task. `NSOperationQueue` controls the execution of `NSOperation` objects through a queuing system. `NSTask` enables the creation and management of processes within the Objective-C runtime. `NSThread` is used to create and control threads. The Appendix includes general guidelines on concurrent programming and the use of threads.

Notifications Support

The Notifications Support classes provide APIs for messaging based on notifications, a message sent to one or more observing objects in response to an event that occurs within a program. The architecture follows a broadcast model; objects receiving events are decoupled from those sending them. `NSNotification` encapsulates the information sent by a notification object; it consists of a unique name, the posting object, and (optionally) a dictionary of supplementary information. The `NSNotificationCenter` and `NSDistributedNotificationCenter` classes provide the mechanisms for broadcasting notifications to interested observers. `NSNotificationQueue` objects act as buffers for notification centers.

Classes that **receive** notification events (i.e., observers) must implement a *notification handler* method with the signature

- (void)**methodName:**(NSNotification *)notif;

An object *(orderHandler)* that implements a notification handler method named `handleOrder` subscribes to notification messages (of type `OrderNotification`) by sending the following message to a notification center (Note that here we are using the default notification center)

```
[[NSNotificationCenter defaultCenter]
  addObserver:orderHandler
  selector:@selector(handleOrder)
  name:OrderNotification object:nil];
```

Classes that **send** notification events create notification instances
and post them to a notification center. The next code fragment
creates a notification instance named `orderNotif`. It is of type
`OrderNotification` (a custom subclass of `NSNotification`),
identified with the name `COC_Order1`, and is sent to observers with
an Order object named `order1`.

```
OrderNotification *orderNotif =
  [OrderNotification
  notificationWithName:@"COC_Order1"
  object:order1];
```

Typically, the object sent to observers (in this case `order1`) is the
object associated with the notification. This `OrderNotification`
instance can now be posted to the default notification center with the
statement

```
[[NSNotificationCenter] defaultCenter]
  postNotification:orderNotif];
```

Archiving and Serialization

The Archiving and Serialization classes implement mechanisms for
creating architecture-independent byte streams of object trees (along
with their associated data) that can then be written to a file or
transmitted to another process, potentially over a network. `NSCoder`
declares the interface used to transfer objects and other data items
between memory and some other format. `NSArchiver` and
`NSKeyedArchiver` are used to encode objects for writing to a file or
some other use. `NSUnarchiver` and `NSKeyedUnarchiver` are
used to decode objects from an archive. The
`NSPropertyListSerialization` class provides methods to
serialize and deserialize property lists directly; it also supports
conversion to/from XML or an optimized binary format.

The following code fragment uses the `NSKeyedArchiver`
`archiveRootObject:` method to archive an `NSString` instance
named `greeting` to a file in the current directory named
`greeting.archive`

```
NSString *greeting = @"Hello, world!";
NSString *cwd = [[NSFileManager defaultManager]
```

```
    currentDirectoryPath];
NSString *archivePath = [cwd
    appendString:@"/greeting.archive"];

BOOL result = [NSKeyedArchiver
    archiveRootObject:greeting toFile:archivePath];
```

This archives the entire object tree (i.e. NSString and its subclasses). The next code fragment uses the NSKeyedUnarchiver unarchiveObjectWithFile: method to decode the archived version of *greeting* from the above-specified file (named *archivePath*)

```
NSString *greeting = [NSKeyedUnarchiver
    unarchiveObjectWithFile:archivePath];
```

While the NSArchiver and NSUnarchiver classes (and subclasses) are responsible for encoding/decoding an object tree, the actual data for the object tree (e.g. its properties, other data items, etc.) is written to/read from these byte streams by implementing the NSCoder interface for each object in the tree. Specifically, the class must implement the appropriate encode and decode method(s) as these will be called by the selected NSArchiver/NSUnarchiver instance. The code fragment below encodes and decodes a property named type (that has a key named *type*) for a class that will be archived.

```
- (void)encodeWithCoder:(NSCoder *)coder
{
    [coder encodeObject:self.type forKey:@"type"];
}
- (id)initWithCoder:(NSCoder *)coder
{
    if (self = [super init])
    {
        type = [[coder decodeObjectForKey:@"type"]
            retain];
    }
    return self;
}
```

Language Services

These classes offer general-purpose functionality for developing Objective-C software. The NSAutoreleasePool class is used to support the *classic* (i.e. reference counting) memory management system. An `NSAutoreleasePool` instance contains objects that have received an *autorelease* message; when released it sends a *release* message to each of those objects. `NSClassDescription` provides the interface for obtaining information about a class and its relationships. The `NSException` class supports exception management. Its methods support creating `NSException` instances, querying the instance, throwing exceptions, and getting the exception stack frames. `NSGarbageCollector` provides an interface to the garbage collection system (only available for the Mac OS X platform). The `NSInvocation` and `NSMethodSignature` classes are used to support the Foundation framework's distributed object system. `NSInvocation` is used to invoke methods on distributed objects. `NSMethodSignature` is used to forward messages that a receiving (distributed) object does not respond to, it contains type information for the arguments and return value of a method. `NSUndoManager` is a general-purpose class for recording operations to support undo and redo.

Given a class `MyCalendar` deployed as a distributed object with the method

```
- (BOOL)updateAppointmentsForDate:(NSDate *)aDate;
```

This code creates and configures an `NSInvocation` object for it

```
SEL theSelector =
  @selector(updateAppointmentsForDate:);
NSMethodSignature *aSignature =
  [MyCalendar
  instanceMethodSignatureForSelector:theSelector];
NSInvocation *anInvocation = [NSInvocation
  invocationWithMethodSignature:aSignature];
[anInvocation setSelector:theSelector];
```

The target (`MyCalendar *` instance `userDatebook`) and arguments (`NSDate *` instance `aDate`) are then set

```
[anInvocation setTarget:userDatebook];
[anInvocation setArgument:&todaysDate atIndex:2];
```

Now the `NSInvocation` object can be invoked with the `invoke` message and its corresponding result obtained with the `getReturnValue:` message

```
BOOL result;
[anInvocation invoke];
[anInvocation getReturnValue:&result];
```

Scripting

The Scripting classes support the creation of *scriptable applications* (ones that can be controlled by AppleScript scripts). AppleScript is a scripting language that makes possible direct control of scriptable applications and scriptable parts of the Mac OS. NSScriptCommand and its subclasses implement standard AppleScript commands. NSScriptObjectSpecifier and its subclasses locate scriptable objects. NSScriptCoercionHandler and NSScriptKeyValueCoding perform essential functions related to scripting.

Distributed Objects

The Distributed Objects classes provide functionality for distributed object communication, in essence an object in one process sending a message to an object in a different process. The NSConnection class manages connections between distributed objects in different threads and/or processes. NSDistantObject is a subclass of NSProxy that defines proxies for distributed objects in other threads or processes. The NSProtocolChecker class defines an object that restricts the messages that can be sent to another object (its delegate). A protocol checker acts as a type of proxy that only forwards the messages it receives to its target if they are in its designated protocol. NSDistantObject and NSProtocolChecker are subclasses of NSProxy; all other classes in the Foundation framework descend from the NSObject class.

To **vend** an object (i.e. to make an object instance distributed so that it can be invoked by other applications over a network), the object should first be configured as the root object of an NSConnection instance and the connection should then be registered on the network. The following code fragment vends the helloService object instance and registers it under the name my_HelloService

```
NSConnection *connection = [NSConnection
  defaultConnection];
[connection setRootObject:helloService];
[connection registerName:@"my_HelloService"];
```

Registration makes the distributed object available to remote clients. Note that a run loop for the connection must be running to capture incoming requests for the distributed object. It can be started using the NSRunLoop run method for the current thread

```
[[NSRunLoop currentRunLoop] run];
```

A client can invoke methods on a distributed object by obtaining a proxy for it. The following code fragment obtains a proxy for the `helloService` distributed object on the local host

```
id proxy = [[NSConnection
  rootProxyForConnectionWithRegisteredName:
    @"my_HelloService"
  host:nil] retain];
```

If `helloService` adopts a protocol named `HelloProtocol` and these are the methods available for clients of the `helloService` distributed object, then the following statement should be used to configure the proxy to support this protocol

```
[proxy setProtocolForProxy:
  @protocol(HelloProtocol)];
```

The Distributed Object classes are only available for use on the Mac OS X platform.

Application Kit Framework

The Application Kit (AppKit) framework consists of a set of APIs that can be used for developing graphical user interfaces for Mac OS X applications: windows, panels, buttons, menus, scrollers, and text fields. There are over 125 classes and protocols in the AppKit framework. Apple provides several ways to use the AppKit classes to develop user interfaces (Interface Builder (IB), create AppKit instances, subclass AppKit classes), depending upon the user interface requirements.

Xcode IB is used to graphically develop user interfaces with AppKit. As you drag and drop your UI components onto the IB canvas and set their properties, it automatically instantiates and configures the corresponding AppKit class instances. You can then implement the application class methods, specifically action and delegate methods, to perform the desired user interface logic. This is the simplest method for using the AppKit to build a user interface, and requires less familiarity with the AppKit classes and protocols.

Another approach is to create and configure AppKit class instances directly to build the user interface in code. This requires more familiarity with the AppKit classes and protocols, but enables dynamic, programmatic control of the user interface.

Finally, it is possible to create custom user interface objects by subclassing AppKit classes such as `NSView`. This enables the developer to write custom methods, but requires a thorough understanding of the AppKit framework.

The Apple AppKit Framework Reference provides detailed documentation for each AppKit API. The framework classes are grouped into the following functional categories:

- User Interface
  These classes provide general user interface management and control. This includes UI application control, event handling, window management, drawing on views, view management and display, menus, and cursors.

- Text Processing
  The text processing classes support text view and manipulation.

- Font Management
  The font classes encapsulate and manage font families, sizes, and variations.

- Graphics
  The graphics classes encapsulate graphics data, its access, and its presentation on screen.

- Color Support
  The color classes support management of color formats and representations.

- Document Support
  These classes provide functionality for window data representation as documents and document I/O via files.

- Printing Services
  The printing services deliver support for printing windows and views, and creating an EPS representation of a view.

- Operating System Services
  These classes implement operating system level functionality, including cut-copy-paste functionality, online help, spell checking, speech recognition, audio support, and workspace support.

- Interface Builder Support
  These classes extend support for integration with Interface Builder nib files.

UI Kit Framework

The UI Kit framework consists of a set of APIs that can be used for developing user interfaces for Mac iOS (iPhone, iPod, iPad) applications. The Apple UI Kit Framework Reference includes detailed documentation for each UI Kit API. The classes are grouped into the following functional categories:

- User Interface
  The user interface classes deliver general user interface management and control for iOS devices. This includes UI application control, event handling, window management, drawing on views, view management and display, menus, and cursors.

- Gesture Recognizer
  These classes provide event-handling support for common gestures that users make on their device's surface, such as triple-tap, touch-and-hold (also called long press), pinching, and rotating gestures. It also provides a framework for the creation of custom gesture recognizers.

- Print Formatting
  The print formatting classes implement functionality for printing of content from iOS devices to local printers. The printing API also enables the printing of content from within custom-developed (user) iOS applications.

- Responder
  The UIResponder class provides the interface for objects that respond to and handle events. It is the superclass for the UI view controller, view, and application class hierarchies.

Appendix

The Appendix supplies further details on the language and several of the key framework classes, along with some recommendations for application development. Example code is also provided to help clarify usage.

Language Elements

Variable Names

Objective-C variables names begin with a letter or underscore, and can then be followed by any combination of letters [a-z, A-Z], underscores, or digits [0-9]. The letters are case sensitive; in addition, a variable name cannot be an Objective-C keyword. Here are some examples of valid variable names

```
counter
_myVar
```

Here are examples of invalid variable names

```
var?
2var
int
```

The first (`var?`) uses an invalid character for a variable name (?), the second (`2var`) begins with a number, and the third is a reserved word (`int`).

Comments

Comments provide a mechanism for documenting code in order to facilitate comprehension by anyone who needs to read it. Objective-C provides mechanisms to support both single line and multi-line comments.

Single Line Comments

The `//` marker identifies text following (on the same line) as comment text, it will be ignored by the compiler. The marker can be placed anywhere on a line, hence single line comments provide a good mechanism for describing what that particular line of code does. The following code fragment includes a single line comment at the end of a line.

```
NSLog(@"Greetings, earthlings!"); // Print message
```

Multi-Line Comments

Comments that extend over multiple lines use the markers `/*` and `*/` respectively. Everything between these two markers is considered a comment and is ignored by the compiler, regardless of where the markers appear on a line. Here is an example multi-line comment.

```
/*
 * This is a multi-line comment
 */
```

Other Types

Enumeration Type

The enumeration type provides a means of creating a set of named integer constants. An enumeration is declared using the syntax

```
enum tagname { var1, var2, ... };
```

where `enum` is the *enum* keyword, `tagname` declares the specific enumeration type, and the integer constants (`var1`, `var2`, `...`) are provided within ellipses. The following code declares an enumeration for playing card suits.

```
enum cardsuit
{
  CLUBS,
  DIAMONDS,
  HEARTS,
  SPADES
};
```

The next code fragment declares an enumeration for the type vehicle_wheels and explicitly sets the value for each of the enumeration constants.

```
enum vehicle_wheels
{
  UNICYCLE = 1,
  BICYCLE = 2,
  TRICYCLE = 3,
  AUTOMOBILE = 4
};
```

You can then declare an instance of this enumeration type and set the instance to a specific value (4 in this example) with this code fragment

```
enum vehicle_wheels wheels;
wheels = AUTOMOBILE;
```

typedef

The typedef keyword is used to create new names (identifiers) for a specific type. They provide a level of abstraction from the actual types being used, and can make code more clear and easier to maintain. A typedef is declared in a statement by providing the typedef keyword, the specific type, followed by the identifier. The statement below declares the identifier whole_number_t to be another name for the unsigned int type

```
typedef unsigned int whole_number_t;
```

Constants

A constant is a data element that has a fixed value that cannot be changed. Constants have a type, name, and value. A constant must be initialized at the same time that it is declared using the const keyword, for example the statement

```
const int n1 = 1;
```

Defines a constant (n1) with a value of 1; if you try to change the value of the constant elsewhere in the code a compile-time error will be reported.

Operators

Assignment Operator

The assignment operator (=) assigns the result of an expression to a variable. Objective-C provides two types of assignment operators, basic and compound. The *basic* assignment operator performs a simple assignment of a variable to the left of the operator to an expression to the right of the variable

```
int myInt = 1;
```

The **compound** assignment operator combines an assignment with an arithmetic or logical operation. For example, the statement

```
mySum = mySum + 2;
```

can be simplified by using a compound assignment operator that combines addition and assignment

```
mySum += 2;
```

Assignment operators can also be chained to assign the same value to multiple variables. The code fragment

```
int nProtons, nNeutrons, nElectrons;
nProtons = nNeutrons = nElectrons = 1;
```

assigns the value of *1* to the variables nProtons, nNeutrons, and nElectrons.

Arithmetic Operators

The arithmetic operators are used for creating mathematical expressions. Arithmetic operators take either one or two operands, and multiple can be used in a single expression. The table below lists the Objective-C arithmetic operators

−	-n1	Negates the value of a variable or expression
+	n1 + n2	Adds the two operands
−	n1 - n2	Subtracts operand n2 from n1
*	n1 * n2	Multiples the two operands
/	n1 / n2	Divides operand n1 by n2
%	n1 % n2	Returns the remainder of operand n1 divided by n2

Table 1. Arithmetic Operators

The following statement multiplies two values and stores the result in the variable *product*

```
int product = 3 * 4;
```

The next example adds three values and stores the result in the variable `sum`

```
int sum = 5 + 8 + 13;
```

Particularly for expressions with multiple operators, it is important to note that Objective-C evaluates expressions according to *operator precedence;* this topic will be discussed shortly.

Increment and Decrement Operators

The increment (++) and decrement (--) operators provide a means of incrementing (or decrementing) the value of a variable by 1. They operate on a single operand. An increment/decrement operator can be placed either before (pre-increment/decrement) or after (post-increment/decrement) the variable name. If it is placed before the variable name the increment/decrement is performed before any other operations are performed on the variable. For example, in the following code fragment

```
int counter = 0;
int totalCount = ++counter;
```

the value of `counter` is incremented before it is assigned to `totalCount`, thus the value of `totalCount` after this assignment is 1;

Logical Comparison Operators

The logical comparison operators perform a comparison of an expression and return a Boolean `YES`/`true` (1) or `NO`/`false` (0) result depending on the result of the comparison. The expression requires two operands. Each logical comparison operators is listed below, along with an example and description

==	n1 == n2	Returns true if n1 is equal to n2
>	n1 > n2	Returns true if n1 is greater than n2
>=	n1 >= n2	Returns true if n1 is greater than or equal to n2
<	n1 < n2	Returns true if n1 is less than n2
<=	n1 <= n2	Returns true if n1 is less than or equal to n2
!=	n1 != n2	Returns true if n1 is not equal to n2

Table 2. Logical Comparison Operators

The following code fragment stores a Boolean value of true (1) in the variable isBigger.

```
int n1 = 50;
int n2 = 25;
BOOL isBigger = n1 > n2;
```

Logical Boolean Operators

The logical Boolean operators also return a Boolean true *(1)* or false *(0)* result; they differ from the logical comparison operators in that they take Boolean values as operands.

!	!n1	Inverts the current value of the operand.
&&	n1 && n2	Returns true if both operands evaluate to true.
||	n1 || n2	Returns true if one or both of its operands evaluates to true.
^	n1 ^ n2	Returns true if one and only one of the two operands evaluates to true.

Table 3. Logical Boolean Operators

The following statement stores a Boolean value of true in the variable isBiggerAndPositive because the two operand expressions evaluate to a value of true

```
BOOL isBiggerAndPositive = (n1 > n2) && (n1 > 0);
```

Ternary Operator

The ternary operator provides a means of evaluating an expression as a function of the evaluation of a condition. The syntax of the operator is

```
[condition] ? [true expression] : [false expression]
```

If the condition evaluates to `true` then the *true expression* is evaluated, otherwise the *false expression* is evaluated. The following code fragment

```
int testNumber = 5;
NSString *result = (testNumber >= 0) ?
  @"Positive" : @"Negative";
```

causes the variable `result` to be assigned the string `Positive`, because the conditional expression (`testNumber >= 0`) evaluates to `true`.

Bitwise Operators

The bitwise operators enable bitwise operations on binary numbers. Any decimal number can be represented as a binary number. The bitwise operators are of two types: comparison and shift. The bitwise comparison operators can perform bit-by-bit comparisons of two numbers, and shifts of each bit in a binary number. These operators return a binary number consistent with the operation. The bitwise shift operators shift each bit in a binary number the specified number of positions.

The bitwise `AND` (`&`) operator uses the `AND` operation to perform a bit-by-bit comparison of two numbers. In each position of the binary sequence for the two numbers an `AND` operation is performed; if both bits are 1 then a 1 is set in the same position of the resulting number, else a zero is set. For example a bitwise `AND` operation on the following two numbers (14 [binary `1110`], and 13 [binary `1101`]) would yield a binary result of `1100` (12 in decimal).

```
int num1 = 14;
int num2 = 13;
int num12And = num1 & num2;
```

The bitwise `OR` (`|`) operator uses the `OR` operation to perform a bit-by-bit comparison of two numbers; it sets a 1 in the same position of the resulting number if there is a one in that position for either (or both) operand. For the following code fragment

```
int num1 = 14;
int num2 = 13;
int num12Or = num1 | num2;
```

the result (`num12Or`) would be set to a (binary) value of `1111` (15 in decimal).

The bitwise XOR (^) operator (also known as the exclusive-or) uses the XOR operation to perform a bit-by-bit comparison of two numbers; it sets a 1 in the same position of the resulting number if there is a one in that position for one and only one of the operands, otherwise the bit is set to 0. For the following code fragment

```
int num1 = 14;
int num2 = 13;
int num12Xor = num1 ^ num2;
```

the result (num12Xor) would be set to a (binary) value of 0011 (3 in decimal).

The bitwise **left shift** (<<) operator moves each bit in a binary number the specified number of positions to the left. As the bits are shifted to the left, zeroes are placed in the right most (vacated) positions, and the left most (high order) bits are discarded if the shift exceeds the size of the variable containing the value. The expression

```
14 << 1
```

Shifts the value 14 (binary 00001110) 1 bit to the left, resulting in a value of 28 (binary 00011100).

The bitwise **right shift** (>>) operator moves each bit in a binary number the specified number of positions to the right. The right most (lower order) bits that are shifted off are discarded. The right shift is a *logical* right shift, because the left most (higher order) bit positions that have been vacated while right shifting are replaced with zeros. The expression

```
15 >> 1
```

shifts the value 15 (binary 1111) 1 bit to the right, resulting in a value of 7 (binary 0111).

The bitwise operators can be combined with the assignment operator. For example, the statement

```
mySum = mySum << 1;
```

can be simplified with a compound bitwise operator

```
mySum <<= 1;
```

The bitwise **one's complement** (~) operator is used to flip the bits of a binary number. Each bit of the number that is one is changed to a zero, and each bit that is a zero is changed to a one. The expression

```
int flip5 = ~5;
```

performs a one's complement of the number 5 (binary `0101`), returning a value of 10 (binary `1010`) for the variable `flip5`.

Type Cast Operator

The type cast (`type`) operator enables a variable to behave as a different type. The type that a variable is cast to is provided within parentheses next to the variable to be cast. Type casting of a variable does not change its type or the value stored. This code fragment

```
int n1Int = 1;
float n1Float = (float)n1Int;
```

casts the variable `n1Int` to a `float`, and assigns this value (1.0) to the variable `n1Float`.

sizeof Operator

The `sizeof` operator provides the length in bytes for an input variable, written in parentheses after the operator. The following code fragment

```
int myArray[2] = {0, 1};
int myLen = sizeof(myArray);
```

returns a value of 8 for `myLen` – each integer is 4 bytes in length, hence the resulting value.

Address Operator

The address (`&`) operator returns the address in memory for a variable (also referred to as its *reference*). The syntax for using the address operator is

```
&varName
```

where `varName` is the name of the variable. The following code fragment

```
int n1Int = 1;
int *n1Pointer = &n1Int;
```

sets the variable `n1Pointer` of type `int` `*` (pointer to an `int`) to the address of `n1Int`.

Indirection Operator

The indirection (*) operator returns the value of a variable pointed to (i.e., it *dereferences* a pointer). The code fragment

```
int sum = *n1Pointer + 2;
```

gets the value pointed to by `n1Pointer` (i.e, 1) and adds it to 2, storing the result (= 3) in the variable `sum`. Note that when used with a single operand in a statement (not a type declaration), the * symbol indicates use of the indirection operator.

Comma Operator

The comma (,) operator has two operands; it evaluates the first operand and discards the result, then evaluates the second operand and returns its value (and type). The code fragment

```
int n1 = 1;
int n2 = 2;
int myNum = (n1, n2);
```

defines and initializes the variables `n1` and `n2`, then defines the variable `myNum` and initializes it to 2 (the value of `n2`).

The comma is also used as a separator for variable declarations, method declarations and definitions, object messaging, and other areas.

Operator Precedence and Associativity

Now that we have looked at the Objective-C operators, we need to understand how operators are evaluated in expression, specifically the order in which operators are evaluated when there is more than one operator in an expression. For example, given the following code

```
int num1 = 10;
int num2 = 20;
int num3 = 30;
int total = num1 * num2 + num3;
```

How should the expression `num1 * num2 + num3` be evaluated? The results will be different depending upon whether the multiplication is done first or the addition is done first. The rules governing expression evaluation in these cases are known as the *operator precedence and associativity* rules. Objective-C operators are grouped together at different precedence levels. Operators of higher precedence are evaluated before operators of lower precedence. When operators at the same precedence level are found within a single expression, the corresponding *associativity* rule determines the order in which the operators are evaluated. Given these general guidelines, the following table defines the operator precedence groups and associativity rules for Objective-C.

Operator	Description	Precedence	Associativity
[]	Access array element or message expression	Highest	
()	Access object member or method		Left-to-right
.	Invoke a method or function		
->	Pointer to structure member		
++	Increment		
--	Decrement		
+	Unary plus		
-	Unary minus		
!	Logical NOT		Right-to-left
~	Ones complement		
*	Indirection (pointer reference)		
&	Address (of)		
sizeof	Size of (object)		
(type)	Type cast		
*			
/			
%	Arithmetic		Left-to-right
+			
-			
<<	Bitwise shift		Left-to-right
>>			
<			
<=			
>=			
>	Logical comparison		Left-to-right
==			
!=			
&			
^	Bitwise comparison		Left-to-right
|			
&&	Logical boolean		Left-to-right
||			
?:	Ternary		Right-to-left
= += -=			
*= /= %=			
&= ^= |=	Assignment		Right-to-left
<<= >>= >>>=			
,	Comma	Lowest	Right-to-left

Table 4. Operator Precedence and Associativity

Due to of the number of rules and groups, it is **highly recommended** that parentheses be used to control the order of evaluation of an expression. This will eliminate coding errors and reduce confusion or mistakes interpreting expressions that have multiple operators. In other words, in the example presented above if the addition of variables `num2` and `num3` should be done first, the expression should be grouped with parentheses as follows

```
int total = num1 * (num2 + num3);
```

Expression Statements

Objective-C uses *statements* to specify programming logic to be executed. An expression statement consists of an expression to be evaluated followed by a terminating semicolon. Expressions can use operators and may contain message passing and function calls.

Conditional Statements

The `if`, `if-else`, `if-else-if`, and `switch` constructs are utilized for program flow control. The `if` statement is used to control execution of program code by specifying logic to be performed if a single Boolean expression evaluates to true. The syntax for the `if` construct is

```
if (Boolean expression)
{
    Conditional logic
}
```

The conditional logic in the body of the statement is only executed if the Boolean expression evaluates to `true`; otherwise it is skipped. The body of the conditional logic is enclosed in braces. If there is only one line of code for the conditional logic the braces are optional (but recommended).

The `if-else` statement augments the `if` statement by specifying code to be executed if a single Boolean expression evaluates to either `true` *or* `false`. The syntax for the `if-else` construct is

```
if (Boolean expression)
{
    True conditional logic
}
else
{
    False conditional logic
}
```

The *True conditional logic* is executed if the Boolean expression evaluates to true, otherwise the *False conditional logic* is executed.

The `if-else-if` statement augments the `if` statement by controlling execution of code based on multiple Boolean expressions. The syntax for the `if-else-if` construct is

```
if (Boolean expression 1)
{
  Conditional logic 1
}
else if (Boolean expression 2)
{
  Conditional logic 2
}.
else if (Boolean expression n)
{
  Conditional logic n
}
else
{
   False conditional logic
}
```

This code would be executed as follows: *Conditional logic 1* is executed if *(Boolean expression 1)* evaluates to `true`, else *Conditional logic 2* is executed if *(Boolean expression 2)* evaluates to `true`, else *Conditional logic n* is executed if *(Boolean expression n)* evaluates to `true`, otherwise the *False conditional logic* is executed if all of the above Boolean expressions evaluate to `false`. Note that if multiple Boolean expressions within the `if-else-if` construct evaluate to `true`, only the conditional logic for the first will be executed.

The `switch` construct enables conditional comparison and execution of code against a wide range of constant values. The syntax for the `switch` statement is

```
switch (expression)
{

  case constant-expression1:

    match1 logic

    break;

  case constant-expression2:

    match2 logic

    break;

  default:

    default logic

    break;

}
```

In a switch statement *expression* is either a value or an expression that returns a value. The *case constant-expression* values represent each possible matching value for the expression. If a case constant-expression matches the value of the expression, the accompanying statements (i.e., the match logic) are executed. After the match statements are executed the break statement is provided to exit the switch statement block. If a break statement is not provided then every case after the matching case is executed - this causes multiple sets of match logic to be executed. The default case is executed if none of the cases match the expression. The type of the switch expression and case constant-expression values must be integral (i.e., int or char). The value of each case constant-expression must be unique within the switch statement body.

Loop Statements

Objective-C has several statements that control looping, i.e. repetitive execution of program logic according to a specific condition(s). The for statement enables the repeated execution of code until an optional condition becomes false. The syntax of the for statement is

```
for (initial-expr; conditional-expr; loop-expr)
{

  Loop logic

}
```

The optional *initial-expr* can be of any type and specifies initialization for the loop. Here you typically initialize variables used during the loop logic and for expression evaluation. The optional Boolean *conditional-expr* is evaluated before each iteration. If the *conditional-expr* evaluates to `true` the loop logic is executed, then the optional *loop-expr* is evaluated. If the *conditional-expr* evaluates to `false` the loop logic is not executed and the loop statement is exited, with program execution continuing at the next statement. If a *conditional-expr* is not provided it is considered `true`, and the loop logic is executed. In this scenario the loop logic would continue to be performed until a `break`, a `goto` (to a labeled statement outside the *for* statement), or a `return` statement is executed. As shown above the body of the loop logic is enclosed in braces. If there is only one line of code for the loop logic the braces are optional (but recommended). `for` loops can be nested, enabling one loop to reside in another loop.

A special form of the `for` loop, the `for...in` loop (also known as fast enumeration), can be used to execute loop logic over a collection of objects. The syntax for the loop is

```
for (type varName in enumeration-expr)
{
    Loop logic
}
```

The iterating variable `varName` is set to each item returned from *enumeration-expr* in turn and the loop logic is executed. The enumeration expression returns an object that conforms to the `NSFastEnumeration` protocol (for example, Foundation framework collection classes such as `NSArray`, `NSDictionary`, etc.).

The `while` statement enables repetitive evaluation and execution of program logic while a specified Boolean expression evaluates to `true`. The syntax for the `while` statement is

```
while (conditional-expr)
{
    Loop logic
}
```

The expression is evaluated, if it evaluates to `true` the loop logic in the body of the while statement is executed, and the process is repeated. If the expression evaluates to `false`, the program exits the `while` statement and continues at the next statement. The `while` statement would also be exited if a `break`, a `goto` (to a labeled statement outside the `while` statement), or a `return` statement is executed within the statement body.

The `do-while` statement provides repetitive execution then evaluation of program logic. It differs from the `while` statement in that the program logic is guaranteed to be executed at least once. The expression in a `do-while` statement is evaluated after the loop logic in the body of the statement is executed. The syntax for the `do-while` statement is

```
do
{
  Loop logic
} while (conditional-expr)
```

The `do-while` statement would also be exited if a `break`, a `goto` (to a labeled statement outside the `do-while` statement), or a `return` statement is executed within the statement body.

Jump Statements

Objective-C has several statements that transfer control unconditionally. The `return` statement terminates execution of a method or function and returns control to the calling method/function. The `return` statement can also return a value to the calling method/function. The syntax for the `return` statement is

```
return expression;
```

The optional *expression* value is returned to the calling method/function and is converted to the type returned by the method/function.

The `break` statement terminates the execution of the nearest enclosing `for`, `while`, `do-while`, or `switch` statement in which it appears. The program continues execution at the statement that follows the terminated statement.

The `continue` statement passes control to the next iteration of the nearest enclosing loop (`for`, `while`, `do-while`) statement in which it appears, bypassing any remaining statements in the statement body. The `continue` statement must appear within a loop statement.

The `goto` statement transfers control to a label that must reside in the same method/function and can appear before only one statement in that same method/function. The syntax for the `goto` statement is

```
goto label;
```

where *label* is an identifier in the current method/function. Control (i.e. the flow of program execution) transfers to the labeled statement.

Understanding Variable Scope

Block Scope

A variable declared within a statement block has *block scope*. Curly braces `{ }` encapsulate a statement block. Variables declared within a block are only visible and accessible within this block. In addition, block-level scope means that a variable can have the same name in different blocks. Any attempt to access a variable defined within a block from outside of the block will result in a compile-time error.

Method Scope

Variables declared within a method have *method scope*. As would be expected, these variables are only visible and accessible within the associated method.

Object Scope

Object instance variables are declared within the corresponding class interface and are accessible according to their access modifiers. Instance variables have an implicit namespace, meaning that they can have the same name within different methods.

File Scope

A variable that has *file scope* is accessible *only* to code within the file where the variable is declared. Variables at file scope can have the same name within different files.

Global Scope

A variable that has *global scope* is accessible both within the file where it has been declared, and also potentially by other files in the Objective-C program. Global variables are declared *outside* of any statement blocks and are typically placed near the top of a source file. To make such a variable accessible in another file it must be declared using the `extern` keyword. This tells the file that this variable is defined elsewhere but is accessible here.

Using NULL, nil, and NSNull

`NULL`, `nil`, and `NSNull` are used often in Objective-C code and the framework classes for various purposes. It is therefore important to understand what they represent, the differences between them, and their proper usage.

`NULL` is a generic pointer type (`void *`) whose value is `0x0`. `NULL` is used where a generic pointer type with no value is required, for example as a method parameter value whose type is `void *`.

The `nil` object is an object (of type `id`) whose value is also `0x0`. As `nil` is an object whereas `NULL` is not, you can send messages to `nil` – calling a method on `nil` will not cause the program to crash. `nil` is also often used in a class `dealloc` method

```
- (void) dealloc
{
  self.myObj = nil;
  [super dealloc];
}
```

This causes the setter method for the `myObj` instance variable (invoked because we used the `self.varName` syntax) to release the old value and retain `nil`, insuring that the `myObj` variable will not be pointing at random data where an object used to be.

`NSNull` is a Foundation framework singleton object used to represent null values where `nil` is not allowed (e.g., with collection objects). Invoking the `null` method on `NSNull`

```
[NSNull null];
```

Returns the singleton instance of `NSNull`.

String Constants versus String Literals

A string literal object (i.e., an `NSString` instance) is an immutable (unchangeable) string value. It is typically created using the following syntax

```
@"Hello, world!"
```

The string value (`Hello, world!`) is placed within a pair of double-quotes and the indirection operator @ retrieves a pointer to the string literal. The above string literal can be assigned to an `NSString *` object named *greeting* with the statement

```
NSString *greeting = @"Hello, world!";
```

Note that this creates an instance of the string `Hello, world!` but does not control occurrences of this string – in other words, if another `NSString *` object, this time called salutation, is created with the same string

```
NSString *salutation = @"Hello, world!";
```

Another string literal is created. Hence the program can have multiple occurrences of the same string. This side effect may be undesirable, particularly for iOS devices with limited memory. A string constant, on the other hand, controls the number of instances of an immutable string. It is declared in a header file, for example

```
extern NSString *const HELLO;
```

then defined in an implementation file

```
NSString *const HELLO = @"Hello, world!";
```

This creates an immutable (unchangeable) string with a constant (unchangeable) pointer to it. Now each assignment of this string, e.g.

```
NSString *greeting = HELLO;
NSString *salutation = HELLO;
```

uses the same pointer, and hence there is only one occurrence of the `Hello, world!` string in memory, even if the program is distributed across multiple files. To create a private string constant that is only visible and accessible in a single implementation file, the `static` keyword should be used

```
static NSString *const HELLO = @"Hello, world!";
```

This guarantees that the string is only visible within the file and there is only one instance of it.

Memory Management and Object Ownership

Classic memory management is implemented by following a set of object ownership rules, whose overriding guideline is *only release objects you own*. An Objective-C program takes and releases ownership of multiple objects throughout program execution, and there can be multiple owners of an object. As long as an object has at least one owner, it continues to exist. If an object has no owners the runtime system destroys it automatically and its memory is reclaimed.

The runtime uses a *retain count* to enable control of object creation and destruction. Each object has a retain count; this indicates the number of owners (i.e. those with an ownership interest) of an object. Once all owners have released their ownership interest on an object, the runtime system sends a `dealloc` message to the object then reclaims its memory. The `dealloc` method should free the object's own memory and dispose of any resources it holds, including ownership of any object instance variables. If the class of an object is defined such that it owns one or more object instance variables, then the `dealloc` method for the class should be implemented to release them and then invoke the `dealloc` method for its parent class.

An Objective-C program manually takes ownership of an object when it either: 1) **creates an object** instance using a method beginning with `alloc`, `new`, `copy`, or `mutableCopy`, or 2) **takes ownership** of an object (i.e. keeps it alive) by sending it a `retain` message.

The program manually releases ownership of an object when it **releases an object** by sending it a `release` or `autorelease` message to the object.

The program should be implemented such that it relinquishes ownership of objects it owns when it is finished with them, and does not relinquish ownership of objects it does not own.

The *autorelease* mechanism is provided to simplify classic memory management. It is comprised of autorelease *pools* and an API, the `autorelease` method defined by `NSObject`, which marks an object for later release. An autorelease pool is an instance of `NSAutoreleasePool` that contains references to objects that have received an `autorelease` message. When an autorelease pool is deallocated, it sends a `release` message to all objects in the pool. This guarantees that the object will be disposed of when it is no longer needed, but can still be safely used within its scope. This eliminates the need to release an object manually and potential errors in releasing an object when it is still needed.

An autorelease pool is created using `alloc` and `init` messages and disposed of using the `drain` message, as shown in the following method

```
int main(int argc, const char *argv[])
{
  NSAutoreleasePool *pool =
    [[NSAutoreleasePool alloc] init];
  NSString *hello = @"Hello, world!";
  NSLog(@"%W", hello);
  [pool drain];
}
```

Autorelease pools are nested – when a new autorelease pool is created, it is added to the top of the stack. When it is deallocated, it is removed from the stack.

To reduce peak memory footprint, it is recommended to create nested autorelease pools and/or release objects manually. For example, if many objects and/or large objects are created in a loop that is executed multiple times, the autorelease pools should be created and disposed of within the loop

```
int main(int argc, const char *argv[])
{
  NSAutoreleasePool *pool =
    [[NSAutoreleasePool alloc] init];
  NSString *hello = @"Hello, world!";
  NSLog(@"%W", hello);
  NSArray *dictionary =
    [[NSFile *dictionaryName] read];
  for (NSString *words in dictionary)
  {
    NSAutoreleasePool *wordPool =
      [[NSAutoreleasePool alloc] init];
    /* Create and release more objects */
    [wordPool drain];
  }
  [pool drain];
}
```

Nested autorelease pools are arranged on a stack, with the "innermost" autorelease pool being on top of the stack. The scope of an autorelease pool is thus defined by both its position in the stack and its existence. Autorelease objects are added to the current topmost pool, if an autorelease pool that is not at the top of the stack is drained, it causes all (unreleased) autorelease pools above it to be drained, along with its objects.

Using ARC

Automatic Reference Counting (ARC) is a new capability added to the Mac Objective-C platform that implements automatic memory management for Objective-C objects and blocks. With traditional (i.e. classical) memory management the Objective-C runtime uses reference counting to control object lifetime – hence the developer must write code that explicitly manages object lifetime via `retain`, `release`, and `autorelease` methods. ARC still uses reference counting, but automatically adds the necessary `retain`, `release`, and `autorelease` calls during program compilation, thus reducing the amount of code written. In addition, application performance is (potentially) improved and errors associated with memory management (e.g. releasing an object that is still in use, retaining an object no longer in use) are eliminated. In addition, as opposed to garbage collection technology ARC is deterministic (the statements are inserted at compile-time) and doesn't introduce pauses into program execution for garbage collection.

Applications can be developed to use ARC on Xcode 4.2 using Mac OS X v10.6 (iOS application development) or Mac OS X v10.7 (Mac application development); it also requires use of the LLVM v3.0 compiler. Applications that use ARC can be deployed on iOS 4 devices or Mac computers with a 64-bit processor(s) running OS X v10.6.

ARC can be used across a project or on a per-file basis if there is a need for manual reference counting in some cases. Apple has also provided a conversion tool (available with Xcode 4.2) that migrates existing code that uses manual memory management to ARC, and also helps you manually convert code that cannot be automatically migrated. ARC is the Apple-recommended method for memory management on new Objective-C projects.

When using ARC in your code there are several new rules for object memory management that must be followed:

- **Object Management**

  You cannot explicitly invoke `dealloc`, or implement or invoke `retain`, `release`, `retainCount`, or `autorelease`. This includes using `@selector(retain)`, `@selector(release)`, and related methods. You may implement a `dealloc` method to manage resources other than instance variables. You **cannot** release instance variables, but you may need to invoke `[systemClassInstance setDelegate:nil]` on system classes and other code that isn't compiled using ARC. Custom `dealloc` methods in ARC **cannot** call `[super dealloc]` (this would cause a compiler error). The chaining to `super` is automated and enforced by the compiler. You can still use `CFRetain`, `CFRelease`, and other related functions with Core Foundation-style objects.

- **Property Parameters**

  The `assign/retain/copy` parameters are no longer used with the `@property` directive. Instead the `weak/strong` parameters are used to tell the compiler how properties should be treated.

- **Object Allocation**

  You **cannot** use `NSAllocateObject` or `NSDeallocateObject` to create objects; you create objects using `alloc` and the Objective-C runtime takes care of deallocating them.

- **Object Pointers in C Structures**

  You cannot use object pointers in C structures, instead use an Objective-C class to manage the data.

- **Casting Between `id` and `void *`**

  There is no casual casting between `id` and `void *`. You must use special casts that tell the compiler about object lifetime. You need to do this to cast between Objective-C objects and Core Foundation types that you pass as function arguments.

- **NSAutoreleasePools**

  You cannot use `NSAutoreleasePool` objects. ARC provides `@autoreleasepool` blocks instead. These have an advantage of being more efficient than `NSAutoreleasePool`. In the case(s) where you still need an autorelease pool (for example, to manage autoreleased objects like certain Foundation framework objects [`NSStrings`, etc.]), it is recommended to use `@autoreleasepool` blocks.

- **Memory Zones**

  You cannot use memory zones (specifically, `NSZone`), as they are ignored by the Objective-C runtime.

- **Method Naming**

  You cannot give a property a name that begins with `new`; this enables ARC code to interoperate with code that uses classical memory management.

- **Exception Handling**

  By default ARC is not exception-safe: it does not end the lifetime of `__strong` variables whose scope is abnormally terminated by an exception, and it does not perform releases of objects which would occur at the end of a full-expression if that full-expression throws an exception. The compiler option `-fobjc-arc-exceptions` can be used to enable exception handling for ARC code. ARC does end the lifetimes of `__weak` objects when an exception terminates their scope unless exceptions are disabled in the compiler.

New qualifiers have also been introduced for regular variables:

- `__strong` – means that any object created using `alloc/init` is retained for the lifetime of its current scope. This is the default setting for variables. The "current scope" usually means the braces in which the variable is declared (i.e. a method, for loop, if block, etc.)

- `__weak` – means the object can be destroyed at anytime. This is only useful if the object is somehow strongly referenced somewhere else. When destroyed, a variable with `__weak` is set to `nil`.

- `__unsafe_unretained` – is just like `__weak` but the pointer is not set to nil when the object is deallocated. Instead the pointer is left dangling (i.e. it no longer points to anything useful).

- `__autoreleasing`, not to be confused with calling `autorelease` on an object before returning it from a method, this is used for passing objects by reference.

For new projects these qualifiers are generally not needed for regular variables, they will more likely be seen with Objective-C code migrated to ARC using the migration tool.

The following pages show the example program listed earlier (in Figures 12-14), updated with ARC memory management.

```objc
//
//  OrderItem.h
//  OrderItem
//
//  Created by Keith Lee on 1/21/12.
//  Copyright (c) 2012 Personal. All rights reserved.
//

#import <Foundation/Foundation.h>

@interface OrderItem : NSObject
{
  @private NSString *comment;
  @private float price;
}

@property (nonatomic, strong) NSString *comment;
@property float price;

- (id) initWithComment:(NSString *)cmt price:(float)cost;
@end
```

Figure 16. OrderItem Interface

The property `comment` is declared with the `strong` attribute, this is functionally equivalent to `retain`.

```
//
//  OrderItem.m
//  OrderItem
//
//  Created by Keith Lee on 1/21/12.
//  Copyright (c) 2012 Personal. All rights reserved.
//

#import "OrderItem.h"

@implementation OrderItem

@synthesize comment, price;

- (id) initWithComment:(NSString *)cmt price:(float)cost
{
  self = [super init];
  if (self)
  {
    [self setComment:cmt];
    [self setPrice:cost];
  }
  return self;
}
@end
```

Figure 17. OrderItem Implementation

Note that the `OrderItem` class does not implement the `dealloc` method; using ARC the compiler automatically inserts the appropriate release calls and also calls `[super dealloc]` as necessary.

```
//
//  main.m
//  OrderItem
//
//  Created by Keith Lee on 1/21/12.
//  Copyright (c) 2012 Personal. All rights reserved.
//

#import <Foundation/Foundation.h>
#import "OrderItem.h"

int main (int argc, const char * argv[])
{
  @autoreleasepool
  {
    OrderItem *item1 = [[OrderItem alloc] initWithComment:@"Hamburger"
      price:3.50];
    OrderItem *item2 = [[OrderItem alloc] initWithComment:@"Hot dog"
      price:2.75];
    NSLog(@"First item is a %@ for $%.2f", item1.comment, item1.price);
    NSLog(@"Second item is a %@ for $%.2f", item2.comment, item2.price);
  }
  return 0;
}
```

Figure 18. main() Function for OrderItem

Notice the use of an `@autoreleasepool` block and the absence of `release` calls for the `OrderItem` objects, these will be automatically added by the compiler.

Understanding Properties

Property attributes provide additional details about the storage semantics and other behaviors of a property. The most commonly used are:

- `readwrite`
  The property can be read or written to. The getter and setter methods must be implemented.

- `readonly`
  This property can be read but not written to. Only the getter method for the property is implemented.

- `assign`
  The setter method uses simple assignment (i.e. not `copy` or `retain`).

- `copy`
  In the setter method a `copy` method should be called for

assignment and the old value should be sent a `release` message.

- `retain`
  In the setter method the previous value will be sent a `release` message and the property uses retain on assignment.

- `strong`
  The `strong` attribute (used when ARC memory management is applied on a property) is equivalent to the `retain` attribute.

- `weak`
  The `weak` attribute (used when ARC memory management is applied on a property) is similar to the `assign` attribute except that if the affected property instance is deallocated, its value is set to `nil`.

- `getter=getterName`
  Renames the getter method to the specified `getterName`.

- `setter=setterName`
  Renames the setter method to the specified `setterName`.

- `nonatomic`
  Specifies that the accessor methods for this property are not *atomic* (the default). The *nonatomic* property setting has better performance, but does not guarantee that a whole value is always returned from a property getter or setter when being accessed by multiple threads.

Properties are typically declared within a class interface, but can also be declared within a protocol or category declaration. As class instance variables are only declared in an interface, the interface declaration must be accessible (perhaps via a `#import` directive to include the class interface file) to make a property declaration in a protocol or category declaration.

The `self` keyword enables access to properties (via the corresponding property methods) within a class definition and is the recommended approach (rather than accessing a property directly). The `super` keyword provides the same capabilities for accessing properties within the parent class definition.

Objective-C properties can be accessed by message passing syntax, dot notation, or by name. Dot notation syntax specifies a dot surround by the object instance name and the property name.

`objectName.propertyName`

This expression provides get/set access to an object's properties. For example, the statement

```
myObject.n1Int = 1;
```

sets the `n1Int` property of the object instance `myObject` to a value of 1. The statement

```
int myValue = myObject.n1Int;
```

Gets the value of the `n1Int` property from `myObject` and assigns it to the variable `myValue`.

Property access by name refers to the `valueForKey:` and `setValue:forKey:` methods provided for any objects that are *key-value coding* compliant (that adopt the `NSKeyValueCoding` protocol, i.e. any properties declared using the `@property` keyword and defined using the `@synthesize` keyword). The above examples can be rewritten with these methods as follows

```
[myObject setValue:1 forKey:n1Int];
```

This sets the `n1Int` property of the object instance `myObject` to a value of 1.

```
int myValue = [myObject valueForKey:n1Int];
```

Gets the value of the `n1Int` property from `myObject` and assigns it to the variable `myValue`.

Using Categories

There are several constraints to keep in mind when using categories. You cannot use a category to add any new instance variables to the class, only new methods. There is no type checking at compile time or runtime to determine whether an object conforms to an informal protocol. Also, there is no limit to the number of categories you can add to a class, but each category name must be different, and each should declare and define a different set of methods.

A category can add methods to any class, including the root (`NSObject`) class. This must be handled with care to guard against unintended changes to unseen classes. Others may be working on the application and are unaware of the changes; this can cause unintended side effects. In addition, when implementing category methods for the root class messages to `super` are invalid and class objects can perform instance methods defined in the root class (normally class objects can only perform class methods).

Message Selectors

A message selector is an identifier that represents a method at runtime. It is a variable of type `SEL` and can be created at either compile time or at runtime. Given a method defined as follows

```
- (NSString *)getGreeting;
```

A compile time selector is created by applying the `@selector` directive on a method name as shown in the following statement

```
SEL greetingSelector = @selector(getGreeting);
```

This statement creates a selector named `greetingSelector` for the `getGreeting` method. A runtime selector is created using the Foundation framework `NSSelectorFromString` function on a string

```
NSString *greetingMethod = @"getGreeting";
SEL greetingSelector =
  NSSelectorFromString(greetingMethod);
```

Selectors define method names, not implementations. The `getGreeting` method in one class has the same selector as the `getGreeting` method defined in other classes, thereby enabling polymorphism and dynamic binding. Hence except for messages sent to statically typed receivers, dynamic binding requires all implementations of identically named methods to have the same return type and the same parameter types. Identically named class methods and instance methods can have different parameter types and return types.

The `NSObject` methods `performSelector:`, `performSelector:withObject:`, and `performSelector:withObject:withObject:` invoke methods defined by message selectors. The following code fragment invokes the `getGreeting` method on an object instance named `hello`.

```
NSString *hi = [hello
  performSelector:greetingSelector];
```

Combined with dynamic typing, it is possible to vary both the message receiver and the message at runtime, variable names can be used in both expressions

```
id messageReceiver = [self getTheReceiver];
SEL messageSelector = [self getTheSelector];
[messageReceiver performSelector:messageSelector];
```

In the above code fragment, the receiver is determined at runtime (by the `getTheReceiver` method) along with the message (by the `getTheSelector` method).

Forwarding Declarations

A forward class declaration provides a means for identifying to the Objective-C compiler that a class exists without specifying its signature (i.e., its methods, properties, etc.). This enables the creation of member variables of this class without having to include the full class declaration (via an import or include file). Forward declarations are useful in a variety of scenarios, in particular for resolving circular dependencies. The `@class` directive is the simplest way to give a forward declaration of a class name. It avoids potential problems that may come with importing files that import still other files. For example, if one class (Class A) declares a statically typed instance variable of another class (Class B), and their two interface files import each other, neither class may compile correctly. A forward declaration in this scenario would be implemented as follows:

1. In the Class A (interface) header file, forward declare Class B. You can then declare a Class B member variable and there is no need to import the Class B header file.
2. In the Class B header file, forward declare Class A. There is then no need for the Class B header file to import the Class A header file.
3. In the implementation file for each class, `#import` the header file(s) for any classes you send messages to (in this case, the Class A and Class B header files).

Handling Errors

The Objective-C language and the Foundation framework together include multiple mechanisms for managing program errors, ranging from simple error codes up to exception handling. In general, errors should be used for handling foreseeable problems that could/should be presented to the user (i.e., when the user may need to fix the problem), while exceptions are used to handle truly exceptional conditions that typically indicate a problem within a program (i.e., to catch a mistake in your code). Also note that the Cocoa frameworks (Foundation, AppKit, UIKit) are not exception safe, hence error codes and error objects must be used for error handling with these APIs.

Error Codes

Error codes and error strings are used to identify (and perhaps convey information) about a particular error that occurs during program execution. An error code is an integer value. This is the simplest mechanism for handling errors but has many issues (it is limited in the amount of information it can provide, is not extensible, causes the mixing of error handling code with solution logic, and is difficult to maintain).

Error Objects

The Foundation framework `NSError` class is used to both encapsulate and convey information about runtime errors that users need to know about. The `NSError` properties are the error code, the error domain, and a dictionary of user information. The error code is a signed integer value. Error codes for the Mac OS X are separated into error domains; useful for identifying the affected Mac OS X subsystem and also distinguishing error codes from different subsystems with the same value. Standard error codes have been predefined for the major error domains, for example under the Cocoa error domain there are predefined Foundation error codes, Application Kit error codes, and Core Data error codes. The user info dictionary holds error information beyond the code and domain. The types of information that can be stored in this dictionary include localized error information and references to supporting objects.

The Application Kit provides APIs and mechanisms that can be used to respond to errors encapsulated in `NSError` objects. The `NSResponder` class defines an error responder chain used to pass events and action messages up the view hierarchy. It includes methods to display information in the associated `NSError` object, and then forwards the error message to the next responder. This enables each object in the hierarchy to handle the error appropriately, perhaps by adding supplemental information pertaining to the error.

The `NSError` class also provides a mechanism for recovering from errors. The `NSErrorRecoveryAttempting` protocol provides methods that are implemented to perform error recovery. An object which adopts the `NSErrorRecoveryAttempting` protocol must implement at least one of its two specified methods. An `NSError` object holds a reference to this object in its user info dictionary. The recovery attempter may implement any logic appropriate for error recovery.

Exception Handling

Objective-C provides mechanisms for handling exception conditions during program execution. An exception condition can be defined as an unrecoverable programming or runtime error. Examples include programming errors such as an unimplemented (abstract) method, or runtime errors such as an out-of-bounds collection access. The compiler directives `@try`, `@catch`, `@throw`, and `@finally` provide runtime support for exception handling, and the `NSException` class encapsulates information pertinent to an exception. When an exception is thrown, resources that are not automatically managed (e.g. Foundation framework objects, objects created using manual reference counting, and any C language-specific resources such as structures) may not be cleaned up properly. Hence no attempt at recovery should be made and the application should be exited promptly.

The `@try`, `@catch`, and `@finally` directives make up a control structure for code that executes within the boundaries of the exception handling logic. The `@try` directive defines a block of code that is within an exception-handling domain, i.e. that can potentially throw an exception. The `@catch` directive defines a block containing code for handling an exception thrown within the preceding `@try` block. The parameter of the `@catch` is the exception object thrown locally, usually an `NSException` object. The `@finally` directive defines a block of related code that is subsequently executed whether or not the associated exception is thrown. The `@throw` directive is used to throw an exception, usually an `NSException` object. When an exception is thrown within the body of an `@try` block, the program jumps immediately to the `@catch` block to handle the exception (if one exists) and then to the `@finally` block.

The Cocoa frameworks come with a large set of predefined exception names that describe specific error states. These should be used (where applicable) when creating an exception.

Assertions

Assertions are used to test assumptions in code. Assertions help verify that the implementation code matches expectations. For example, the following statement

```
NSAssert(myObject != NULL, "Object is NULL");
```

asserts that the variable `myObject` is not null; if it is, an assertion error is thrown. There are two categories of assertion macros available: those for use in Objective-C methods (`NSAssert`, `NSAssert1`, and `NSParameterAssert`), and those for use in functions (`NSCAssert` and `NSCParameterAssert`). These macros evaluate a condition and, if the result is false, they pass a string describing the failure to their associated `NSAssertionHandler`. The `NSAssertionHandler` prints an error message that includes the method and class (or function) containing the assertion and then raises an exception.

Concurrent Programming

Concurrent programming is the development of software organized as collections of interacting tasks that may be executed in parallel. Writing effective concurrent programming logic can be difficult, due to a variety of factors such as the inherent support provided by the underlying system for concurrency, synchronization between multiple tasks, sequencing of communication, and coordinating access to shared resources. Mac OS X and iOS offer several general mechanisms for concurrent programming: threads and asynchronous tasks.

Threads

The Foundation framework `NSThread` class can be used for managing thread instances. Methods on `NSObject` are used for creating new threads and executing code on running threads. The following statement returns the current thread of execution

```
NSThread *current = [NSThread currentThread];
```

For an object `helloService` with a method `getGreeting`, the following statement uses the `performSelectorInBackground:withObject:` method (inherited from `NSObject`) to invoke `getGreeting` in a separate, background thread

```
[helloService performSelectorInBackground:
  @selector(getGreeting) withObject:nil];
```

Operation Queues

An operation queue is an Objective-C object that provides the ability to execute tasks concurrently. Each task (i.e. operation) defines the work to be performed along with its associated data; it is encapsulated in either a **block** or a subclass of NSOperation. An NSOperationQueue object is used to manage execution of the operation. Operation queues may employ threads to execute their operations; however this implementation detail is hidden, thereby simplifying application development and reducing the potential for errors. The code fragment below defines a concrete subclass of NSOperation (HelloNSOperation) that contains the code to perform the given task

```
@implementation HelloNSOperation
- (void) main
{
  NSString *hello = @"Hello, world!";
  NSLog(@"%@", hello);
}
@end
```

An instance of this operation can then be submitted to an NSOperationQueue to execute concurrently

```
NSOperation *helloOp =
  [[HelloNSOperation alloc] init]
NSOperationQueue *theQueue =
  [NSOperationQueue mainQueue];
[theQueue addOperation:helloOp];
```

The preceding paragraph stated that a task could be encapsulated in either a **block** or a subclass of NSOperation, so let's talk a little about blocks and how they are used. **Block objects** are a C language feature (introduced in Mac OS X v10.6 and iOS 4.0) that is similar to function pointers conceptually, but have some additional benefits. Instead of defining blocks in their own lexical scope, you typically define blocks inside another function or method so that they can access other variables from that function or method. Blocks can also be moved out of their original scope and copied onto the heap, which is what happens when you submit them to a dispatch queue. All of these semantics make it possible to implement very dynamic tasks with relatively little code. The following section includes a detailed overview of blocks and how to use them in your code.

Operation queues provide a simpler, more efficient mechanism for implementing concurrency, and hence should be used in lieu of threads for implementing concurrent programming in Objective-C.

Dispatch Queues

A dispatch queue is a C language based mechanism that provides the ability to execute tasks either serially or concurrently. Dispatch queues are typically implemented using Grand Central Dispatch (GCD), a collection of language features, runtime libraries, and system enhancements to support concurrent programming at the operating system level.

Blocks

Blocks provide a way to create a function body as an expression and assign that expression to a variable. They are similar to standard C functions, but in addition to executable code they may also contain variable bindings to stack or heap memory. A block is an implementation of a *closure,* a function that allows access to variables outside its typical scope. They were developed as an extension to the C family of programming languages (C, Objective-C, and C++) and are available with Mac OS X v10.6 and later, as well as iOS 4.0 and later.

Blocks are most naturally used to implement small, self-contained pieces of code that encapsulate units of work. They may be executed concurrently, over the items of a collection, or as a callback when an operation has finished. Blocks differ from traditional callback functions in that they can be written at the point of invocation and executed later in the context of the method, and they also allow access to local variables.

Syntax

The syntax for a block *reference* variable declaration is

```
returnType (^blockName) (arguments);
```

Where `returnType` is the type of the value returned by the block expression, the `^` declares a block variable named `blockName` (`^blockName` is enclosed in parentheses), and `arguments` (also enclosed in parentheses) are the arguments passed to the block for execution. Here is the declaration of a block variable named `simpleBlock` that has a single `int` argument

```
int (^simpleBlock)(int);
```

The syntax for a block definition is

```
^(argumentType, argumentsName, …) { statements };
```

Where ^ indicates this is a block definition with 0 to many arguments (the arguments are enclosed in parentheses with a type and a name for each, separated by commas), and the `statements` are the block code to be executed (the statements are enclosed within ellipses). An example implementation of the above block variable would be

```
simpleBlock = ^(int anInt)
{
  return anInt - 1;
};
```

The declaration and definition can be combined in one statement

```
int (^simpleBlock)(int) = ^(int anInt)
{
  return anInt - 1;
};
```

Usage

You can invoke the block just like you would a function; i.e. by specifying the name followed by the argument values in parentheses

```
int value = simpleBlock(6);
```

As a block reference is a variable it can also be used as an argument to a method or function

```
unsigned int (^decrement)(unsigned int) =
^(unsigned int anInt)
{
  return anInt - 1;
};

NSString *hello = @"Hello, world!";
NSString *fragment = [hello
substringToIndex:decrement([hello length])];
NSLog(@"String Fragment is %@", fragment);
```

A block can also be defined inline as a method or function argument; in this case the return type of the block is inferred from the return statement. I mentioned earlier that blocks are closures; what this means is that, in effect, a block has access to local variables that are in scope when it is defined. These local variables will be treated as constants when the block is executed. For example, the following code fragment

```
int offset = 4;
int (^adder)(int) = ^(int anInt)
{
   return anInt + offset;
};
NSLog(@"Total is %d", adder(1));
```

will print a value of 5 (= 4 + 1). However, if the code is extended as follows

```
int offset = 4;
int (^adder)(int) = ^(int anInt)
{
   return anInt + offset;
};
offset = 10;
NSLog(@"Total is %d", adder(1));
```

It still prints a value of 5; this is because at the time of definition the variable offset has a value of 4, and hence that is the value used when the block is executed. Blocks support the following types of variables:

- Global variables, including static local variables.
- Local variables and parameters from an enclosing scope; typically the lexical scope of a block is delimited by the nearest enclosing ellipses for a statement/group of statements.
- Block variables (those declared with the storage type __block). These can be changed within the block (and the enclosing scope) and are preserved if any referencing block is copied to the heap.
- const imports.

Using a block variable, the following code fragment adds the input amount to the block variable value

```
__block int value = 4;
void (^addToValue)(int) = ^(int anInt)
{
   value += anInt;
   NSLog(@"Added %d to number, its value is now
        %d", anInt, value);
}
addToValue(1);
```

Within a method implementation, blocks can access (Objective-C) instance variables.

Block Objects

An Objective-C a block is actually an object; it is a subclass of NSObject and has all of its associated properties (you can send messages to it, etc.). At runtime a block is allocated on the stack and thus has the same lifetime as a local variable. As a result you cannot use a block outside of the scope in which it is defined. If you need to extend the lifetime of a block, for example if you want to return it from a method or save it for later use, then the block must be moved into permanent storage (i.e., copied onto the heap) and subsequently released when no longer in use, as shown in the following code fragment.

```
typedef int (^Adder)(int);
@interface AdderBlock : NSObject
{
   int addend;
}
@property int addend;
- (Adder) getAdder;
@end

@implementation AdderBlock
@synthesize addend;
- (Adder)
{
   return [[ ^(int anInt)
   {
      return (anInt + addend);
   } copy] autorelease];
}
@end

int main(int argc, const char * argv[])
{
   NSAutoreleasePool *pool = [[NSAutoreleasePool
      alloc] init];
   AdderBlock block = [[AdderBlock alloc] init];
   [block setAddend:4];
   Adder adder = [block getAdder];
   NSLog(@"Sum = %d", adder(1));
   [block release];
   [pool drain];
   return 0;
}
```

Without the `copy` call the `Adder` block would no longer be available after it's returned from the `getAdder` method invocation. The `autorelease` call releases the block after the program is no longer using it. With traditional (manual release/retain) memory management you must manually control block lifetime with the appropriate copy and release method invocations, as shown above. With ARC memory management, the compiler automatically performs the block copy and release operations as long as the block does not return an `id` type or pass an `id` type as a parameter (in either case, the copy and release operations must be performed manually, as before).

Blocks include support for Objective-C object instances, and other blocks, as variables. By default if a block uses an object instance, even if it just uses an instance variable of the object, the object is retained within the block (i.e., the block takes an ownership interest in the object). However, if an object instance is declared with the `__block` storage type, it *is not* retained if used within a block. In other words, for the code fragment

```
NSNumber *offset = [NSNumber numberWithInt:4];
int (^adder)(int) = ^(int anInt)
{
   return anInt + [offset intValue];
};
NSLog(@"Total is %i", adder(1));
```

The `adder` block retains the `offset` object during block invocation. Note that when using ARC memory management, the `__block` storage type **does** automatically retain object instances within a block, thus to avoid circular references to these objects you should declare them with the `__weak` storage type.

NSObject Methods

`NSObject` is the root class of most Objective-C class hierarchies. From `NSObject`, other classes inherit a basic interface to the run-time system for the Objective-C language. Some of the key methods of the `NSObject` class are presented in the following paragraphs.

Object Creation

+ (id) `alloc` – allocates memory for the receiving object and initializing all of its instance variables to zero. It returns a pointer to the receiving object. The object is stored in the default memory zone.

+ (id) `allocWithZone` – performs the same function as the `alloc` method, storing the object in the memory zone specified as an input parameter to the method.

– (id) `init` – initializes the object after memory has been allocated for it.

+ (id) `new` – a convenience method that performs the `alloc` and `init` methods in a single statement.

– (void) `dealloc` – performs any cleanup work required before the object is freed from memory. The `dealloc` method is called by the runtime when there are no longer any references to the object.

– (void) `finalize` – invoked by the garbage collector on an object before it releases the memory the object uses. This method is invoked instead of the `dealloc` method (when garbage collection is enabled).

Class Initialization

+ (void) `initialize` – initializes a class before it is used. This message is sent by the runtime to each class in a program just once, before the class (or any class that inherits from it) is sent its first message from within the program. This method is implemented to perform any class-specific initialization required.

+ (void) `load` – invoked whenever a class or category is added to the Objective-C runtime. This message is sent to classes and categories that are both dynamically loaded and statically linked; it is implemented to perform any class-specific behavior upon loading.

General Purpose

– (id) `self` – returns the receiving object.

+ (NSString *) `description` – returns a string description that describes the contents of the class.

– (BOOL) `isEqual:`(id)anObject – returns boolean `true` if the receiver and the given input object are equal, else returns `false`.

– (NSUInteger) `hash` – returns an integer that can be used as a table address in a hash table structure.

Memory Management

- `(id) autorelease` – Adds the receiver to the current autorelease pool. The *autorelease* mechanism is used with classic memory management.

- `(id) retain` – Increments the receiver's reference count. This message is used for reference counting with classic memory management.

- `(NSUInteger) retainCount` – returns the receiver's reference count. This method does not account for any pending *autorelease* messages sent to the receiver.

- `(oneway void) release` – Decrements the receiver's reference count. This message is used for reference counting with classic memory management.

Class Information and Introspection

+ `(Class) class` – Returns the class object.

+ `(Class) superclass` – Returns the class object for the receiver's parent (class).

- `(BOOL) isSubclassOfClass` – Returns boolean `true` if the class is identical to, or a descendent of the (input) class.

- `(BOOL) isKindOfClass` – Returns boolean `true` if the object is a descendent or member of the (input) class object.

- `(BOOL) isMemberOfClass` – Returns boolean `true` if the object is a member of the (input) class object.

- `(BOOL) isKindOfClass` – Returns boolean `true` if the object is a descendent or member of the (input) class object.

- `(BOOL) instancesRespondToSelector` – Returns boolean `true` if the object can respond to the (input) selector.

- `(BOOL) conformsToProtocol` – Returns boolean `true` if the object conforms to the (input) protocol.

+ `(BOOL) conformsToProtocol` – Returns boolean `true` if the class conforms to the (input) protocol.

Method Information and Introspection

- `(IMP) methodForSelector:(SEL)aSelector` – Instance method that locates and returns the address of a method implementation (the `IMP` type) so it can be called (at runtime) just like a C function.

+ `(IMP) instanceMethodForSelector:(SEL)aSelector` – Class method that locates and returns the address of a method implementation.

- `(NSMethodSignature *) methodSignatureForSelector:(SEL)aSelector` – Instance method that returns a description of the instance method identified by the input selector.

+ `(NSMethodSignature *) instanceMethodSignatureForSelector:(SEL)aSelector` – Class method that returns a description of the instance method identified by the input selector.

- `(BOOL) respondsToSelector:(SEL)aSelector` – Returns boolean `true` if the receiver implements or inherits a method that can respond to the specified message.

Sending Messages

- `(id)performSelector:(SEL)aSelector` – Sends the specified message to the receiver and returns the result of the message.

- `(id)performSelector:(SEL)aSelector withObject:(id)anObject` – Sends a message to the receiver with an object as the argument.

- `(id)performSelector:(SEL)aSelector withObject:(id)anObject withObject:(id)anotherObject` – Sends a message to the receiver with two objects as arguments.

- `(void)performSelector:(SEL)aSelector withObject:(id)anArgument afterDelay:(NSTimeInterval)delay` – Invokes a method of the receiver on the current thread using the default mode, after a delay.

Forwarding Messages

- `(void)forwardInvocation:(NSInvocation *)anInvocation` – Implemented by subclasses to forward messages to other objects.

- `(id)forwardingTargetForSelector:(SEL)aSelector` – Returns the object to which unrecognized messages should first be directed..

- `(void)doesNotRecognizeSelector:(SEL)aSelector` – Handles messages the receiver does not recognize.

Dynamically Resolving Messages

+ `(BOOL)resolveClassMethod:(SEL)name` – Returns boolean *true* if a class can dynamically provide an implementation for a selector of a class method; i.e. the class method is found and added to the class.

+ `(BOOL)resolveInstanceMethod:(SEL)name` – Returns boolean `true` if a class can dynamically provide an implementation for a selector of an instance method; i.e. the method is found and added to the class.

Archiving

+ `(id)awakeAfterUsingCoder:(NSCoder *)aDecoder` – Dynamically provide an implementation for a given selector for a class method.

Class Descriptions

- `(NSArray *)attributeKeys` – Returns an array of NSString objects containing the names of immutable values that instances of the receiver's class contain.

Scripting

- `(FourCharCode)classCode` – Returns the receiver's Apple event type code. A `FourCharCode` is a data type that holds four bytes and is commonly used (via Apple events) for inter-application communication.

Creating a Project in Xcode

The Developer Tools chapter provided a brief overview of Xcode, along with instructions for obtaining the software. Now let's use the IDE to create a project. Start by launching Xcode, the welcome window is presented

Figure 19. Xcode Welcome Window

From here a variety of options are presented, let's select the **Create a new Xcode project** option (Note that you can also create a new project by selecting **File ➜ New ➜ New Project ...** from the Xcode menu).

Figure 20. New Project Assistant

The Xcode IDE window is displayed, and in front of that the *New Project Assistant* pane. The left side of the New Project Assistant is divided into iOS and Mac OS X sections. We are going to start off by creating a command line application, so select **Application** under the Mac OS X section. In the upper-right pane you'll see several icons that represent each of the project templates that are provided as starting points for creating Mac OS X applications, select **Command Line Tool** and click **Next**. A new window will be displayed for you to input project-specific information.

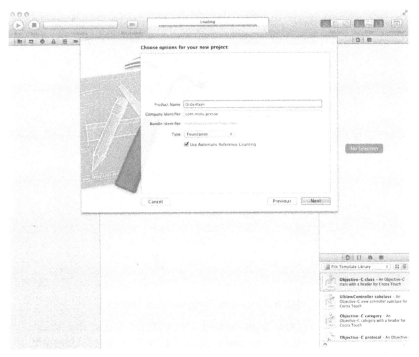

Figure 21. Project Options Window

Specify the *Product Name* for the project (for this example OrderItem), a *Company Identifier* (this is a name used to provide an identifier for your application, typically you input something like your domain name in reverse order but any name will suffice), the *Type* of application (Xcode supports various application types, including C, C++, etc., here we select **Foundation** for an Objective-C project that uses the Foundation framework), and finally a checkbox to specify whether or not the project will use *Automatic Reference Counting* for memory management. After this information has been provided click **Next** and a window is displayed for entering the name and location for the project.

Figure 22. Project Location Window

Specify the folder where you want the project to be created (if necessary select **New Folder** and enter the name and location for the folder), and also select the **Source Control** checkbox if you would like a *git* source code repository to be created for this project. After this has been entered click the **Create** button and the Xcode project window opens.

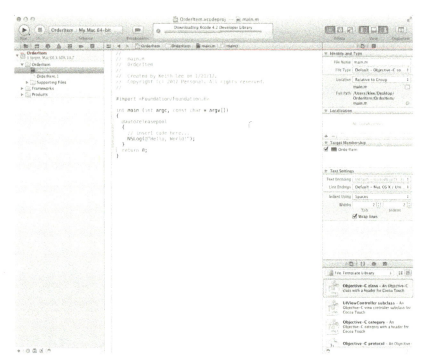

Figure 23. Xcode Project Window

That's it, you have now created an Xcode project! The Apple Xcode 4 User Guide provides a full introduction to Xcode and its features.

Next Steps

Whew! Done with a few minutes to spare. I know that this was a lot to cover in 24 hours, but by reading this book you now have a solid foundation in Objective-C, understand its key features and benefits, and should be ready to begin using it to develop great applications on the Mac. Keep in mind that there are plenty of books and reference guides available to assist you, along with numerous users groups and Objective-C developer communities. The website **http://www.motupresse.com** is a great place to find Objective-C code examples, links to reference guides and documentation, and access book updates and corrections as they become available. Welcome to Objective-C software development using the Mac and enjoy the experience!

Resources

There is a wealth of documentation available, both in print and online, for learning more about Objective-C. There are also numerous mailing lists, discussion forums, blogs, and web sites that provide helpful advice. The next few pages list some of the extensive documentation available on Objective-C programming and the Mac software development tools.

Objective-C

The Objective-C Programming Language:
http://developer.apple.com/library/mac/documentation/Cocoa/Conceptual/ObjectiveC/ObjC.pdf

Object-Oriented Programming With Objective-C:
http://developer.apple.com/library/mac/documentation/Cocoa/Conceptual/OOP_ObjC/OOP_ObjC.pdf

Learning Objective-C: A Primer:
http://developer.apple.com/library/mac/#referencelibrary/GettingStarted/Learning_Objective-C_A_Primer/_index.html#//apple_ref/doc/uid/TP40007594

Apple's Extensions to C:
http://www.open-std.org/jtc1/sc22/wg14/www/docs/n1370.pdf

Transitioning to ARC Release Notes:
http://developer.apple.com/library/mac/#releasenotes/ObjectiveC/RN-TransitioningToARC/_index.html

GNUstep Base Programming Manual:
http://www.gnustep.org/resources/documentation/Developer/Base/ProgrammingManual/manual.pdf

Clang LLVM Automatic Reference Counting:
http://clang.llvm.org/docs/AutomaticReferenceCounting.html

Foundation References

Foundation Framework Reference:
http://developer.apple.com/library/mac/documentation/Cocoa/Reference/Foundation/O
bjC_classic/FoundationObjC.pdf

Foundation Functions Reference:
http://developer.apple.com/library/mac/documentation/Cocoa/Reference/Foundation/M
iscellaneous/Foundation_Functions/Foundation_Functions.pdf

Foundation Data Types Reference:
http://developer.apple.com/library/mac/documentation/Cocoa/Reference/Foundation/M
iscellaneous/Foundation_DataTypes/Foundation_DataTypes.pdf

Foundation Constants Reference:
http://developer.apple.com/library/mac/documentation/Cocoa/Reference/Foundation/M
iscellaneous/Foundation_Constants/Foundation_Constants.pdf

Foundation Programming

Advanced Memory Management Programming Guide:
http://developer.apple.com/library/mac/documentation/Cocoa/Conceptual/MemoryMg
mt/MemoryMgmt.pdf

Archives and Serialization Programming Guide:
http://developer.apple.com/library/mac/documentation/Cocoa/Conceptual/Archiving/Ar
chiving.pdf

Assertions and Logging Programming Guide:
http://developer.apple.com/library/mac/documentation/Cocoa/Conceptual/Assertions/A
ssertions.pdf

Binary Data Programming Guide:
http://developer.apple.com/library/mac/documentation/Cocoa/Conceptual/BinaryData/
BinaryData.pdf

Blocks Programming Topics:
http://developer.apple.com/library/mac/documentation/Cocoa/Conceptual/Blocks/Block
s.pdf

Collections Programming Topics:
http://developer.apple.com/library/mac/documentation/Cocoa/Conce
ptual/Collections/Collections.pdf

Concurrency Programming Guide:
http://developer.apple.com/library/mac/documentation/General/Conceptual/Concurren
cyProgrammingGuide/ConcurrencyProgrammingGuide.pdf

Data and Time Programming Guide:
http://developer.apple.com/library/mac/documentation/Cocoa/Conceptual/DatesAndTi
mes/DatesAndTimes.pdf

Data Formatting Guide:
http://developer.apple.com/library/mac/documentation/Cocoa/Conceptual/DataFormatt
ing/DataFormatting.pdf

Distributed Objects Programming Topics:
http://developer.apple.com/library/mac/documentation/Cocoa/Conceptual/DistrObjects
/DistrObjects.pdf

Error Handling Programming Guide:
http://developer.apple.com/library/mac/documentation/Cocoa/Conceptual/ErrorHandlin
gCocoa/ErrorHandlingCocoa.pdf

Event-Driven XML Programming Guide:
http://developer.apple.com/library/mac/documentation/Cocoa/Conceptual/XMLParsing
/XMLParsing.pdf

Exception Programming Topics:
http://developer.apple.com/library/mac/documentation/Cocoa/Conceptual/Exceptions/
Exceptions.pdf

Garbage Collection Programming Guide:
http://developer.apple.com/library/mac/documentation/Cocoa/Conceptual/GarbageColl
ection/GarbageCollection.pdf

Interacting With the Operating System:
http://developer.apple.com/library/mac/documentation/Cocoa/Conceptual/OperatingSy
stem/OperatingSystem.pdf

Locales Programming Guide:
http://developer.apple.com/library/mac/documentation/CoreFoundation/Conceptual/CF
Locales/CFLocales.pdf

Notification Programming Topics:
http://developer.apple.com/library/mac/documentation/Cocoa/Conceptual/Notifications
/Notifications.pdf

Number and Value Programming Topics:
http://developer.apple.com/library/mac/documentation/Cocoa/Conceptual/Numbersan
dValues/NumbersandValues.pdf

Predicates Programming Guide:
http://developer.apple.com/library/mac/documentation/Cocoa/Conceptual/Predicates/P
redicates.pdf

Preferences and Settings Programming Guide:
http://developer.apple.com/library/mac/documentation/Cocoa/Conceptual/UserDefault
s/UserDefaults.pdf

Stream Programming Guide:
http://developer.apple.com/library/mac/documentation/Cocoa/Conceptual/Streams/Str
eams.pdf

String Programming Guide:
http://developer.apple.com/library/mac/documentation/Cocoa/Conceptual/Strings/Strin
gs.pdf

Threading Programming Guide:
http://developer.apple.com/library/mac/documentation/Cocoa/Conceptual/Multithreadi ng/Multithreading.pdf

Timer Programming Topics:
http://developer.apple.com/library/mac/documentation/Cocoa/Conceptual/Timers/Time rs.pdf

Tree-Based XML Programming Guide:
http://developer.apple.com/library/mac/documentation/Cocoa/Conceptual/NSXML_Co ncepts/NSXML_Concepts.pdf

URL Loading System Programming Guide:
http://developer.apple.com/library/mac/documentation/Cocoa/Conceptual/URLLoading System/URLLoadingSystem.pdf

Xcode

Xcode 4 User Guide
http://developer.apple.com/library/mac/#documentation/ToolsLanguages/Conceptual/ Xcode4UserGuide/Introduction/Introduction.html#//apple_ref/doc/uid/TP40010215

Xcode Quick Start Guide
http://developer.apple.com/library/mac/documentation/IDEs/Conceptual/xcode_quick_ start/Xcode_Quick_Start_Guide.pdf

Xcode Transition Guide
http://developer.apple.com/library/mac/documentation/IDEs/Conceptual/Xcode4Transi tionGuide/Xcode4TransitionGuide.pdf

Xcode 4 Review
http://pilky.me/view/15

Code Coverage in Xcode 4
http://maniacdev.com/xcode-4-tutorial-and-guide/

Cocoa

Cocoa Fundamentals Guide:
http://developer.apple.com/library/mac/documentation/Cocoa/Conceptual/CocoaFund amentals/CocoaFundamentals.pdf

Application Kit Framework Reference:
http://developer.apple.com/library/mac/documentation/Cocoa/Reference/ApplicationKit /ObjC_classic/AppKitObjC.pdf

UI Kit Framework Reference:
http://developer.apple.com/library/ios/documentation/UIKit/Reference/UIKit_Framewor k/UIKit_Framework.pdf

Index

Z